4

TOOLS FOR BUILDI
UNDERSTANDING

D0383366

The GOSPEL *of* GRACE

By DR. MARK WICKSTROM

The GOSPEL *of* GRACE
By Dr. Mark Wickstrom

© copyright 2008 Dr. Mark Wickstrom

All scripture references used in this book are from the
New International Version (NIV) unless listed otherwise.
Lutheran Cyclopedia Concordia Publishing House, St. Louis, MO. P. 343

ISBN 13: 978-1-59298-232-5
ISBN 10: 1-59298-232-8

Library of Congress Catalog Number: 2008926402

Book design and layout: Rick Korab, Punch Design, Inc..
Cover photography: © Jorge Salcedo | Dreamstime.com
Printed in the United States of America

First Printing: June, 2008
Second Printing: March, 2012

16   15   14   13   12   5   4   3   2

Beaver's Pond Press

7108 Ohms Lane
Edina, Minnesota 55439 USA
(952) 829-8818
www.BeaversPondPress.com

To order, visit www.BookHouseFulfillment.com or call
1-800-901-3480. Reseller and special sales discounts available.

CONTENTS

Foreword

Hello Mark,

"The Gospel of Grace"—wow! I so enjoyed reading it and I can't wait to do so again. I learned more through your book than I have in years—fascinating insights, thought provoking and inspiring. I strongly encourage all to read it—this taught me more about tolerance than anything I have yet come across.

I appreciated the exercises at the end of each chapter, encouraging introspection at every turn. I found, at the end, that I walked away with a much greater understanding of those who may interpret the Bible differently than I have been taught—especially important in this day and age, right?

You have such a gift, not just as a biblical scholar, but as a teacher. You tackled some very controversial topics in these case studies, and through your book, I grew to better understand how to bring us together as a people of faith.

Well done!

Blessings,
Diane Nelson

Retail Executive
San Francisco, CA.

Preface

The gestation period for a meadow vole, also known as the field mouse, is twenty-eight days. The gestation period for a human child is roughly nine months. The gestation period for an elephant is nearly two years. The gestation period for this book has been decades. Literally. The seeds were planted years ago as I pondered questions in the Sunday school classes and summer camp experiences of my youth. They lay dormant for a while during my college years, in the turbulent decade of the sixties. Then, the seeds began to gestate during my first seminary experience (I have had two more seminary experiences since then).

After seminary, I received my first call; I became the youth director of a large Congregational church in Edina, Minnesota. What an experience! As our group grew in number, I encountered a hunger and thirst for the Bible that I never dreamed possible. Students were asking good questions—hard questions—and I realized that I had to come up with some answers. Not simple answers, not pat answers, but real, thoughtful, insightful answers. After all, these young people were taking advanced placement tests for college credit, and were competing for National Merit scholarships. They were applying to and entering some of the top colleges and universities in the world. I realized I needed to prepare them for the academic world they were about to enter. So I taught our kids about the different ways to study the Bible: form criticism, the historical-critical method, and the documentary hypothesis (the theory that there is not one author of the Hebrew Testament, but rather there are four distinct strands, labeled JEPD, woven together to make the first five books of the Hebrew Testament). The students listened and questioned, and together we learned some more.

One of my favorite stories from this era is about when one of my former youth group students came to visit me on her first Thanksgiving break from college. She was attending an exclusive East Coast college and she had taken a "Bible as literature" class during her first semester. She smiled as she told me about one particular class meeting. One day during class the professor introduced the documentary hypothesis to the first year students and for some reason he failed to mention the E strand (so-called because of the use of *Elohim*, a Hebrew word for God). My young friend raised her hand and asked why he hadn't included the E strand. Apparently the professor was stunned. He was used to blowing students away and now the table was turned. He admitted that he had made an oversight, and then asked how in the world she knew it existed. "Oh, we talked about it in our youth group," she told him matter-of-factly. A freshman who was not blown away by critical thinking but saw it as a matter of course. . . that had been my goal. That is still the goal of serious biblical teaching.

Over the next few decades my call was as the executive pastor of a large Lutheran church in suburban St. Paul, Minnesota. It was there that I committed to teaching a Bible study every Monday morning. The goal? To teach each of the twenty-seven books of the Greek Testament. Here again, the verse-by-verse, chapter-by-chapter, book-by-book study was meant to encourage the members of the group to ask questions, to ponder deep issues, and to apply the principles that they learned to real life. I am eternally grateful for the students of all ages who faithfully gathered on beautiful fall mornings, freezing cold winter mornings, and rainy spring mornings as we worked our way through the entire Greek Testament. In this atmosphere the seeds of this book grew into a small plant that took root and began to flourish. The concepts in this book went through several mutations, morphing, so to speak, into the way they are presented today. Many of the folks from the Monday morning group encouraged me to write a book about our approach to the Bible, some even promised to buy it if it ever came out. I don't know if they will, but their enthusiasm at the time genuinely inspired me to consider this venture.

Currently I serve as the senior pastor of a large Lutheran church in Las Vegas, Nevada. Here I have had the opportunity to pull all the pieces together, to really water the plant and help it mature. I committed to making the time to put the decades of thoughts and teachings into an organized account. I set aside time to write each week and slowly this manuscript has come together. I offer thanks to God for the journey that has brought me here. I pray that each person who reads this book can become more comfortable with the contents of the library we call the Bible. Like my young friend from years ago who was not intimidated by taking a critical look at the Bible, I hope that you will gain confidence in your use and understanding of God's word.

Dedication

TO MY WIFE, KRISTI, WHO HAS

FAITHFULLY LOVED, LISTENED,

CRITIQUED, AND ENCOURAGED

ME EVERY STEP OF THE WAY.

The Bible: A Library

his book is for anyone who wants to take the Bible seriously. My intention is to provide a forum for every reader of the Bible to have what I never had growing up in the faith: a way of understanding how two people can use the same book to justify conflicting opinions. For example, in the late 1960s I heard committed Christians quote Bible verses, such as Romans 13:1, which states, "Everyone must submit himself to the governing authorities, for there is no authority except that which God has established," to justify the government's issuing of draft notices and their own willingness to go to war and fight the designated enemy in Southeast Asia. In contrast, I heard other committed Christian friends say they could not obey the government draft notice because the Bible says, "Do not repay anyone evil for evil" (Rom. 12:17). People in this camp interpreted the Bible as saying they should not go to war against anyone, even those deemed evil. They insisted war would be returning evil for evil. Both groups of Christians quoted supporting verses from the Bible. Each one said the other camp was wrong. Both factions claimed to have the true biblical perspective. It was perplexing. How could the Bible support opposing opinions at the same time? Is there only one correct biblical interpretation of this issue?

In the years that followed I discovered that many issues garnered conflicting opinions: divorce, abortion, the role of women in ministry, capital punishment, grace, forgiveness, and even baptism, to name but a few. I also observed good Bible-believing Christians espousing conflicting opinions about each issue. It seemed that each side would quote their particular verses and then claim biblical victory, thereby blasting the opposing view. When disagreement persisted, each camp would quote even more verses, and then each would claim that the argument was over. I found this frustrating, and my frustration stemmed from the nagging perception that neither side ever adequately explained how their particular combination of Bible verses really overruled the opposing viewpoint's set of Bible verses. It was then that I set out to determine how to best understand the Bible in terms of its history.

The book we call the Bible is really a library comprised of sixty-six books that are divided into 1,189 chapters. The chapters are subdivided into 31,102 verses. These books were written over one thousand years of human history from roughly 900 BCE ("before the common era") to approximately 100 CE ("of the common era"). Each book, letter, poem, epistle, story, or parable was written by a human author living in a real village or city that was part of a real country, surrounded by real economic and cultural influences that affected the author's life. We Christians believe these people were inspired by the Holy Spirit to write what they wrote. Unfortunately, none of the original manuscripts made it past the second century CE. That means that in the nineteen hundred years since the originals disappeared our versions of the Bible have been passed on by redactors, secretaries (both professional and not professional), and monks (some trained and some not trained) who copied the manuscripts by hand and the copies were passed on to succeeding generations. Since the original manuscripts of the portion of the modern Bible from Genesis to Malachi were written in the Hebrew language, the texts (taken together, Christians call them the Old Testament) were later translated into the academic languages of antiquity, first Greek and then Latin. The text of the Matthew to Revelation scriptures (Christians refer to these collectively as the New Testament) was written originally in Greek, then translated into Latin, and then translated into the Romance languages, German, and finally English. Obviously, not all words can be translated easily or identically into different languages, so all editions of the manuscripts were subject to some human interpretation. Over the centuries certain beliefs have developed about how to interpret the texts we call the Bible. On the one hand, there are the literalists; on the other are the selectivists. Let's take a look at each of their approaches to scripture.

For literalists, the Bible moved through all the centuries and renditions while retaining two important qualities. First and foremost is the Bible's inerrancy. That is, there are no mistakes in any of the texts. For those who claim to be literalists, the Bible says what it says and means what it means. For example, people who claim to take the Bible literally often quote Jesus' words recorded in the Sermon on the Mount in Matthew 5:18: "I tell you the truth, until heaven and earth disappear, not the smallest letter not the least stroke of a pen, will by any means disappear from the Law until everything is accomplished." Literalists take this to mean that not one jot or tittle of the Bible's original Hebrew alphabet will be changed until whatever God wants accomplished is done. If the smallest punctuation marks will not be changed, they argue, certainly there can be no room for mistakes of any more significant magnitude in the Bible.

A second quality literalists treasure is inspiration. The verse most frequently cited to support this point is found in Paul's letter to the young pastor, Timothy. Paul writes, "All scripture is God breathed and is useful for teaching, rebuking, correcting and training in righteousness." (2 Tim. 3:16). The use of the description "God breathed" implies for many literalists that the writing of the Bible was essentially automatic writing, with God dictating to a human author who merely wrote down on papyrus, reed paper, or lambskin the original words issued from God. Given these two core beliefs literalists often take a stand that maintains that every verse in the Bible is equally inspired, equally important, and equally true.

In contrast, selectivists suggest that every verse in the Bible cannot be taken literally. They believe that every author was inspired, but that cultural biases or real life circumstances may have played a role in influencing the writer. Selectivists get their appellation from their practice of selecting some verses to be taken literally and other less important verses not to be taken literally. They highlight verses they perceive have greater value to the life of a child of God and minimize verses they perceive as less important. For example, a humorist put together the following letter:

Dear Bible Believing conservative fundamental literalist,

I have heard you say you take the whole Bible at its word. Would you please shed some of your insight on how to understand the following texts: 1. Leviticus 25:44 states that I may possess slaves, both male and female, provided they are purchased from neighboring nations. A friend of mine claims that this applies to Mexicans, but not Canadians. Can you clarify? Why can't I own Canadians? 2. I know that I am allowed no contact with a woman while she is in her menstrual uncleanness Leviticus 15:19–24. The problem is how do I tell? I have tried asking, but most women take offense. 3. I have a neighbor who insists on working on the Sabbath. Exodus 35:2 clearly states he should be put to death. Am I morally obligated to kill him myself, or should I ask the police to do it? 4. I have a teenage daughter who cursed at me as she went to her room after supper. Leviticus 20:9 directs that she should be put to death. Should I use stoning or strangulation? 5. A friend of mine feels that even though eating shellfish is an abomination-Leviticus 11:10, it is a lesser abomination than homosexuality. I don't agree. Can you settle this? Are there degrees of abomination? I know you have studied these things extensively and thus enjoy considerable expertise in such matters. Thank you again for reminding us that God's word is eternal and unchanging. Sincerely, Mr. Inquisitive.

Mr. Inquisitive has uncovered a number of verses that no Christian would literally put into practice. No parent would be able to quote Leviticus 20:9 as a biblical justification for killing his or her belligerent teen (no matter how many frustrated parents have fantasized about doing it!). Selectivists would say that it is obvious that this verse and others like it are not to be taken in the literal sense. Probably most literalists would agree. However, what process does the reader of the Bible use to determine if one verse warrants literal interpretation while another verse does not? This book is about the process of deciding how we determine our use of any particular biblical text. The technical term used for this process is "hermeneutic," and it entails determining what is meant by a text and how it can be applied in real life. Although the 31,000 verses in the Bible are inspired by God, they are not all given equal importance nor are they treated with equal value by selectivists.

When you get done reading this book you will be able to see and hopefully understand why a person might treat some verses literally and other verses figuratively. It should be apparent that neither literalists nor selectivists treat all biblical passages uniformly. There are certainly verses that literalists will not put into practice. There are also verses that selectivists will interpret literally. The real difference is the degree to which a person chooses literal over selective interpretation . Whichever camp you find yourself in most of the time, you will discover that you have made a choice about every verse. You choose to take some passages literally and you choose to take others figuratively. This book will assist you in understanding which choices you have made and possibly why you made those particular choices.

An additional benefit of reading this book is the opportunity it will afford you to have a more meaningful conversation with a person who has put a verse in a different category. In many settings such conversations become shouting matches, with one or each side denouncing the other. Similarly, the emotions of the moment may reduce the conversation to name-calling or even worse, to a condemnation of the opposing view as unbiblical. With the tools offered in this book, you will be able to comprehend when someone interprets a verse differently than you do.

There is one more important thing to keep in mind. This book is not about me dictating which verses are to be placed in each category. Every reader is free to place any given text where the Holy Spirit of

God leads him or her. I will offer my opinions from time to time but I am more interested in encouraging you to use the tool for yourself than stressing my own view. Whenever appropriate, take time to converse with people who place the same text in another category. I believe a great deal can be learned from such conversations.

© Chance Agrella | Dreamstime.com

Domino Theory
vs. the House Theory

*U*sing the domino theory has been one approach to biblical interpretation for as long as I can remember. The theory is based on the old game of dominos. I remember as a kid standing the rectangular blocks up on their small edges. We would then make long lines and even intricate designs with the blocks. The trick was making sure the individual dominos were close enough together so that when the first one fell over, a chain reaction would result, subsequently knocking down all the remaining dominos, one after the other. The work of setting them up was tedious. The enjoyment was watching each domino knock down its neighbor domino as one long wave.

In the world of literal biblical interpretation, the domino theory suggests that if one verse of the Bible is proven to be wrong, a chain reaction ensues, one that would undermine the authority of the entire Bible as the word of God. For example, in Genesis 1 we find the first story of creation, which opens with "In the beginning God created the heavens and the earth" (Gen. 1:1). The text goes on to describe the orderly six-day creation of the universe, with the seventh day designated for rest. If the Bible says God created the universe in six days, the literalist argument goes, then creation lasted for six twenty-four-hour days. Another might suggest that this seems improbable; surely it would take longer than that to create the universe and everything in it. However, if someone were to cast doubt on the six-day creation, literalists argue, how can we know that any of what the Bible says is true? If the veracity of the Bible's first story is undermined, how can we trust any subsequent story? Why would the author have used the word "day" if he didn't mean twenty-four hours? The literalist conclusion is that readers must trust that what they are reading is God's word. Literalists may also offer this caution from the Greek Testament: "For the time will come when men will not put up with sound doctrine. Instead, to suit their own desires, they will gather around them a great number of teachers to say what their itching ears want to hear. They will turn their ears away from the truth and turn aside to myths" (2 Tim. 4:3–4). In the literalist view, agreeing that "day" means twenty-four hours means accepting the truth. To disagree by suggesting that "day" might mean something else, like "era," would entail turning away from the truth and accepting a myth.

There is a corollary to the domino theory, one suggesting that if no verse is ever wrong, then the word of God can never be undermined. The inerrancy and inspiration of all scripture would be preserved forever. I espoused the literalist domino view as the prevailing way of understanding scripture for years. However, over time I found it to be an inadequate approach to interpreting the Bible. I found that I needed a different understanding. I would never have guessed where the new understanding would originate.

A few years ago my wife and I had the privilege of building a house in Stillwater, Minnesota. What started out as a project meant to give us a new place to live turned into a metaphor that proved to be a surprisingly adequate understanding of how the Bible could be interpreted by a selectivist. Here is what I discovered.

Our house started out as a hole in the ground with footings of poured cement reinforced with rebars of steel. On this foundation the weight of the entire structure would rest. Once the footings were firm, the house was framed with sturdy, treated two-by-fours, two-by-sixes, and two-by-eights. These timbers were locked together with nails as the frame of the house came together. Once the frame was done, the trusses were added for the roof and the skeleton of the house was complete. It was obvious the rest of the house would be dependent on this framework, which had to bear the weight of the entire structure.

The framed, trussed skeleton that sat on the foundation was the backbone of the house. When it comes to biblical interpretation, I believe that what I call "the gospel of grace," wherever it is found in the Bible, is the framework that holds the whole Bible together. The gospel of grace is found in the Hebrew (Old) Testament and in the Greek (New) Testament. The gospel of grace is the primary message God wanted to give all human beings, regardless of gender, race, or nationality. The gospel of grace is the heart of the Bible. Like the frame of our house, the gospel of grace bears the weight of everything else in the Bible. As our Stillwater house moved forward and the frame was set, the internal walls began to go up. These were not necessarily weight-bearing walls, but they were the floor-plan walls that would make our house distinctive from other framed structures in our neighborhood. These unique internal walls I would liken to the Bible texts that I call "timeless truths." Timeless truths are those passages of scripture that are selected by individuals or denominations to be held as timeless truths. These do not have to do with grace, but rather with what makes a person's or denomination's beliefs distinct from those of other Christians or other people who use the Bible as their basis for understanding God and faith. It is important to note that internal walls can be changed (it's called remodeling) and when they are, the whole house does not fall down. So, too, timeless truths can be altered over time and for a variety of reasons, but the biblical house does not collapse. When ideas or interpretations about verses taken as timeless truth change, the biblical house looks different in appearance, but the base of the house is still preserved.

Once the internal walls of our new house were up, we took on the task of decorating the house. Obviously, the style of fixtures we chose, the pile of the carpeting, and the colors selected for the walls each added uniqueness to our house. Similarly, when we do biblical interpretation we refer to passages of scripture that I call "cultural norms" and "personal opinions." These texts contribute to the color and texture to our understandings of the Bible. The verses that we put in each of these categories will reflect the traditions we were exposed to as we grew up or the opinions of people who influenced us on our spiritual journeys. The passages we consider cultural norms may change over time. When you repaint a room in a house or recarpet a section of hallway, the rooms or sections of the house certainly look different, but the interior walls remain standing, and the house is never in danger of falling down. Nor does the house's foundation alter.

So, too, do cultural norms and personal opinions function in biblical interpretation. Verses that are placed in the cultural norm or personal opinion categories can be moved around and the biblical house is still very secure.

With the Stillwater house's structure and interior completed, the last thing we did was move in. We had furniture, artwork, and knick-knacks that all needed to be arranged room by room. Some of the belongings we brought with us didn't fit the decor of the new house, though they had worked nicely in a previous house. If they were family heirlooms, we put them in boxes that we then stored in the basement or the attic above the garage. In the Bible there are some stories and verses that I call "random texts." At their best these are verses or stories that seem to not quite fit the surrounding text, like mismatching pieces of furniture we don't know what to do with. At their worst they are problematic verses appearing to go against the very message of the Bible. We must keep in mind that furniture can be moved, switched out, or even sold and the house does not fall down. It just looks different on the inside. I have uncovered some Bible verses that are confusing at best and at worst darn right baffling, causing us to wonder why they remained in the Bible for over two thousand years. However, they are there and we will deal with some of them. These random texts will not cause the biblical house to tumble down, regardless of what we do with them.

So there was the metaphor I needed, found in an unexpected place. The house of biblical interpretation was framed on the gospel of grace; the internal walls were the distinctive timeless truth texts that I chose; the decorating was accentuated by the verses that were cultural norms and personal opinions; and the inappropriate furniture were those random texts that just didn't seem to belong in the house any longer. Unlike the domino theory, where one verse could undermine the entire Bible, the house analogy demonstrated that the Bible could be treated

with critical thinking, honest evaluation, and even periodic remodeling. The framework of the gospel of grace would be able to support all kinds of floor plans, decorating tastes, and furniture purchases.
This is exactly what I think has happened. The gospel of grace is the inerrant and divinely inspired framework that holds the Bible together. Around that framework has gathered every church, denomination, and individual believer, fashioning his, her, or its biblical house by placing each chapter and verse in the categories of timeless truths, cultural norms, personal opinions, and random texts. Thus, all our houses of faith look distinctive from those of others. They reflect different opinions—different spiritual tastes if you will—yet we all use the same verses to come to different conclusions.

Over the next six chapters we will look at each of these categories in greater detail, and take into consideration specific biblical passages. You are welcome to compare how you categorize these verses to construct your biblical house. My goal is not to tell you where to put your verses, just as I do not need you to tell me where to put mine. In essence, we are each the architect of our own biblical house. Let's take an honest look at how we have designed our individual house first. Then we can compare our choices with people who have made choices that are different from ours. I believe if we allow God's Holy Spirit to lead us we can learn to talk patiently to one another about our similarities and our differences. The beauty in all of this is that the biblical house will not fall down as long as the gospel of grace is the framework that bears the weight of our understanding. Let's look at that important foundational frame next.

© Kirill Putchenko | Dreamstime.com

The Gospel *of* Grace

he frame of our house of biblical interpretation is the gospel of grace. "Grace" is defined in the *Lutheran Cyclopedia* as God's "good will and favor shown to one who can plead no merit to receiving it." I believe grace is found equally in the Hebrew Testament and the Greek Testament, and in the Bible God initiates grace in many different forms. We will look at several of them. We'll see that grace is

God's activity made available to all creation and all created beings. To communicate the gospel of grace is the reason the library of books we call the Bible was written. Let's take a look at where grace originates.

"And the Lord said . . . I will have mercy on whom I will have mercy, and I will have compassion on whom I will have compassion." These words recorded in Exodus 33:19 confirm that God is the initiator of all forms of grace. God shares God's mercy and compassion as God sees fit. God decides what forms grace takes. For example, God's grace takes the form of decent clothes for Adam and Eve as they are escorted out of the Garden of Eden (Gen. 3:21). During the exodus, the experience of God's grace is tangible in the quail and the manna that sustain them daily (Exod. 16:4–12). God's grace comes in the form of an animal in Leviticus 16:20–23, as Aaron casts the sins of all Israel on the head of a goat that is sent into the wilderness. Interestingly enough, this is the origin of the term "scapegoat" (someone who takes the blame for another's failure). God's grace was offered to those who obeyed the sacrificial codes outlined in the Hebrew Testament. The Day of Atonement is available every year on the tenth day of the seventh month of the Hebrew calendar, as outlined in Leviticus 16.

God also determines who receives the grace. God chose to bless Abram as recorded in Genesis 12. Certainly all of Abraham's decedents have been extended God's grace just as he promised Abram. But God has chosen to include other people, too. For example, God chose to extend grace to Rahab, a prostitute working in Jericho who helped the Hebrew spies (Josh. 2). God's grace was extended to Ruth who was a Moabitess (Ruth 1). The whole city of Nineveh was the recipient of God's grace when its inhabitants accepted the message Jonah preached to them (Jon. 3). God's grace was extended to Jews and non-Jews as God saw fit. The same pattern is found in the Christian Testament eight hundred years after Jonah.

God's grace takes human form in the incarnation of Jesus. In his ministry Jesus gave tangible forms of unmerited favor when he healed many (Matt. 8), when he fed thousands (Matt. 14), when he performed miracles (John 2), when he restored life (Matt. 9), and when he forgave sins (Mark 2). In these instances we see Jesus initiating the forms of grace. If we look carefully we see that Jesus was indiscriminate with respect to whom he extended the grace as well. It was offered to a Samaritan woman (John 4), to a Gentile man possessed of a demon (Mark 5), to a Canaanite woman (Matt. 15), to a Jewish official named Nicodemus (John 3), and to a Roman guard (Matt. 8:5-13). These are examples of God extending grace and mercy to whomever God chooses.

After Jesus' ascension into heaven, God's grace is extended to those who received the Holy Spirit at the Pentecost celebration (Acts 2), to the Samaritans through Philip (Acts 8), to an Ethiopian eunuch (Acts 8), to a Roman centurion (Acts 10), to Gentiles in Antioch (Acts 11), to Gentiles and Jews living in cities and regions such as Iconium, Lystra, Derbe, and Syria (Acts 14), as well as in Thessalonica, Berea, Athens (Acts 17), and Corinth and Ephesus (Acts 18, 19). Of course, the gospel of grace was not extended only to the Gentiles and Jews in those remote regions. The followers of Jesus in Jerusalem (Acts 15) played an important role in the intentional spread of the gospel of God's grace to the first-century world.

God's grace is the major message the apostle Paul delivers to the world on his five missionary journeys and in the letters he sends to the churches he started. In Romans 3, Paul informs the early listeners that "no one is righteous, not even one." He goes on to say, "for all have sinned and fall short of the glory of God." But all who believe are "justified freely by his grace through the redemption that came by Christ Jesus." God initiates grace by God's own choice. God gives the grace away freely and without regard to gender, nationality, economic status, political allegiance, race, or educational achievement. Paul summarizes the inclusive nature of God's grace in Romans 9:15–16: "For he says to Moses, 'I will have mercy on whom I have mercy, and I will have compassion on whom I have compassion.' It does not, therefore, depend on man's desire or effort, but on God's mercy." Here, Paul reiterates the Exodus 33:19b text, making it perfectly clear to all his readers that the grace-dispensing God of the Hebrew Testament is the same grace-giving God of the Greek Testament. The gospel of God's incredible, amazing grace is the structure on which the remainder of the Bible rests. That grace is available to men and women, young and old, as well as to people of all nationalities, ethnic origins, and cultural backgrounds. That grace was available in ancient times (Joel 2:28–30), in first-century times (read Ga. 3:26–28), and continues today.

Exercise: If you would like to research what else the Bible says about grace, here are some selected texts to look up. I encourage you to read each text, then consider your responses to the following questions: Who is giving the grace? Who is receiving the grace? What form is the grace taking? Some Hebrew Testament texts include: Gen. 6–7, Deut. 10, Deut. 19, Deut. 21, 2 Kings 4, 1 Sam. 12, Hosea 11 and 14, Amos 9, Jonah, Zeph. 3, and Ps. 130. Now consider some Greek Testament examples: Mark 2:5; Luke 14:15–23; John 5:24–30; John 6:40–47; Acts 10:9; Acts 16; Rom. 3:20–24; Rom. 5:8, 6:14, 11:6, and 11:25ff; Eph. 2:4–6; 2 Cor. 12:9; 1 Pet. 1:23; and James 5:16. Create your own list of Bible verses, stories, parables and teachings that demonstrate grace at work. You may want to create a symbol to put in the margin of your Bible any time you encounter grace being talked about or demonstrated in a text. This would be a great visual reminder of how frequently the framework of grace appears in the Word of God.

And here are some additional questions to consider: Can you describe a time you experienced unmerited favor from a person? Can you think of a time you felt the unmerited favor of God? Can you recall a time you shared unmerited favor with another person? Now read Matthew 6:14–15. How do you interpret Jesus' words as they pertain to extending grace (forgiveness) to another person?

© Max Dimyadi | Dreamstime.com

© Ewa Walicka | Dreamstime.com

Timeless Truths

imeless truths are the internal walls built on top of the framework of the gospel of grace. The verses that we designate as timeless truths provide insight into what people should believe and even how people ought to live and act when they have accepted the gospel of grace. There are some timeless truth verses about which literalists and selectivists might hold common assessments. For example: God is love (Ps. 136, 1 John 4:7–19); God is creative (Gen. 1, Col. 1:15–20); all human beings are subject to temptation (Gen. 3, James 1:12–16); all people sin (1 Kings 8:46, Rom. 3:23); the wages of sin is death (Gen. 2:17, Rom. 6:23); God has the capacity to judge (Deut. 1:17, 2 Tim. 4:1); the Holy Spirit comes from God (Joel 2:28, John 14:16); God wants us to pray (2 Chron. 7:14–15, 1 Thess. 5:17); God wants us to seek him (Deut. 4:29, Matt. 7:7); God cares about the poor (Amos 5:11–15, Matt. 6:2–4); God cares about justice (Mic. 6:8, Luke 11:24); and God wants us to love our neighbors (Lev. 19:18, Matt. 22:39).

As you consider each of the timeless truth texts above, you will notice that the core ideas are found in both the Hebrew and Greek Testaments. I think if these were the only texts we had there would be far less disagreement between different groups attempting to follow God's directives. However, it is the presence of other texts that cause the perceived need for separation. There are other verses throughout the Bible that, when put into the category of timeless truths, cause people to take issue or outright disagree with one another. In other words, certain verses, when made into timeless truths, are used as dividers to distinguish who is on the inside of the wall (i.e., agrees with a point of view) and who is on the outside (i.e., disagrees with a point of view). Quite often people on the inside are quick to condemn those who are on the outside of the wall of their interpretation. The gospel of grace is intact, but the internal walls of separation are quickly built and not very readily taken down. Let's look at some examples of verses that, when they are made into timeless truths, can become walls of separation.

In 1 Timothy 2:9–15 Paul advises women to dress modestly, learn quietly, and not to usurp the authority of the man. Nor should a woman teach a man. Churches that have made this a timeless truth are compelled to follow these directives. When these verses are perceived as timeless truths in the modern world, they can be used in arguments attempting to prevent women from voting, from holding offices in congregations, or from serving as ordained pastors in denominations. These conclusions are all very logical if the supporting verses are interpreted as timeless truths, as backed by the fact that Paul said it and that is what he meant for all time. If, however, a person, church, or denomination interprets this same text as a cultural norm, the verses would not be considered normative for all time. Cultural norms are created by people in response to real but specific situations. For example, Paul may have known a woman in Timothy's church who dressed inappropriately, who was outspoken, or whose presence created trouble. Paul's message to Timothy may have been given to put that particular woman in her place. The apostle may not have perceived that every woman in all future time would need to be quiet and modest. Seeing Paul's directive aimed at a particular person or situation in a specific time and place would make it normative for the culture of Timothy's church, not necessarily for that of all future churches.

Let's look at 1 Corinthians 11:5: "But any woman who prays or prophesies with her head unveiled disgraces her head." In this text Paul demands that women have their heads covered whenever they pray. Growing up in eastern Pennsylvania, I was surrounded by dedicated Christian people who took this text to heart. The literal understanding of this verse as a timeless truth meant the Amish and Mennonite women around Lancaster County wore their hair covered all the time. In 1 Corinthians 11:4 Paul advises "every man who prays or prophesies with his head covered dishonors his head." Obviously Paul did not think men should have their heads covered when they are in the place of prayer. I remember entering St. Mark's Cathedral in Venice, Italy, with a group of pilgrims. The docent for the church stood at the door telling men to take their hats off: no caps or hats were allowed on men in that sacred space. The cathedral took the Pauline text and made it a timeless truth—an imperative meant to be followed—and twenty-first-century men were being told to take off their head coverings.

A few years ago I encountered a young woman who, after hearing the explanation of timeless truths that I presented at a seminar, approached me. She told me she now understood why her church required all their parishioners to take off their shoes when they entered the worship center. She proudly showed me the text in Exodus 3 where Moses encounters God's presence in the burning bush. God instructs Moses, "Remove the sandals from your feet, for the place on which you are standing is holy ground" (Exod. 3:5). For this young lady's denomination, anytime a member entered their worship space they were entering holy ground. Their church had made Exodus 3:5 a timeless truth and everyone who entered dutifully took off his or her shoes. That was the first time I had encountered a group that took that particular text literally. However, because they did, they lived by it.

I have read about groups of Christians who have made an unusual name for themselves because they chose to make Mark 16:18 a timeless truth. On more than one occasion I have read of people who live out their faithfulness by showing the power of God at work in their lives. The text says, "And these signs will accompany those who believe . . . they will pick up snakes with their hands; and when they drink deadly poison, it will not hurt them at all." There have not been too many churches choosing to make the handling of snakes and drinking poison timeless truths. However, when this verse is made a timeless truth, the whole focus of worship takes on a new emphasis. People who make snake handling and drinking poison a timeless truth take the matter seriously and literally. Thankfully that has not been part of my religious tradition. Those who follow this text as a timeless truth uniquely put their very lives on the line every time they put their faith to the test!

The call for baptism would seem to be a unifying text among followers of Christ. Jesus is recorded in Matthew 28:19 as saying, "Therefore go and make disciples of all nations, baptizing them in the name of the

Father and of the Son and of the Holy Spirit" It would appear to be a
practice with universal application. However, baptism is actually
one of the most divisive practices in Christianity. How is that possible,
you ask? Well, different groups call for baptism to be done in different
ways. I remember receiving a tract with the catchy cover title: "What
the Bible says about infant baptism . . ." and upon opening it up, I
found that the inside was blank. The obvious inference was that
baptizing infants was not talked about in the Bible; therefore, it
was not to be done in real life. Christians who have made adult
baptism the timeless truth often refer to the text of Jesus being
baptized as an adult (Mark 1:10). They go on to point out that all the
other disciples came to faith in Jesus as adults. Since it is commonly
assumed that John immersed Jesus bodily in the Jordan River, the
inference was also drawn that all baptisms should be by immersion
(by totally dunking the person under water). Interestingly enough, the
idea that baptism had to be done in a river or specifically the Jordan
River has not been deemed literally necessary.

The church groups that practice baptizing infants, of which I, as a
Lutheran, am a member, often point to a text such as Mark 10:14,
that says, "When Jesus saw this, he was indignant. He said to them
'Let the little children come to me, and do not hinder them, for the
kingdom of God belongs to such as these.'" One might use this passage to argue that baptism is an occasion to bring children to receive
the unmerited favor of God. The younger the child, the less the child
could ever think that he or she did anything to deserve the grace
God was bestowing on him or her. The act of baptism for a newborn,
therefore, can be considered an instance of the unmerited favor of God
given through the water that is used, the words that are spoken, and
the Holy Spirit of God present in the sacrament of that event. Grace,
one might argue, is never more clearly an unmerited gift than when
children do not even know they've received it.

As we can see, baptism in general may be universally acknowledged as a timeless truth, but the verses that separate Christians have to do with how baptism is administered (sprinkling on the forehead or full-body immersion), when baptismal water is applied (as an infant or adult), who should apply the water (ordained clergy or any believer), and where it is done (in a church or any body of water). The verses selected as timeless truths will define how, when, and by whom baptism is handled. Each baptism format is either a wall including people who agree with the practice, or a wall excluding people who disagree. The way baptism is done is a cultural norm adopted by each denomination.

Exercise: Take a look at your congregation's or denomination's statement of beliefs. Then make a list of texts that the group uses as the basis for each of their beliefs. You may want to look up each of the passages and mark them in your own Bible. Here are some more passages over which there often is debate. We might ask: Are these timeless truths or cultural norms? You are welcome to look each one up and determine if it is a timeless truth or cultural norm for you personally or for your church.

I have included Hebrew and Greek Testament references together. Ask yourself the following: What is the topic being addressed? Who is the audience in each setting? Was this a timeless truth for the original reader? Is this a timeless truth for you today? Exod. 20 and Rom. 13; Jonah and Col. 3:11; Ps. 133:1 and John 17:20–23; Ps. 95:6 and Rom. 12:1; Ps. 42:5 and 1 Cor. 15:19; Prov. 4:5 and James 1:5.

And here are some additional questions to ponder: Do you agree with all of your denomination's choices of verses that are claimed as timeless truths? You might want to make a list of verses that you hold as timeless truths. Are there verses that you think are timeless truths that differ from those of your congregation or your denomination?

Using Jesus' baptism as the model, consider why being baptized in a river has not been held as a timeless truth by most people.

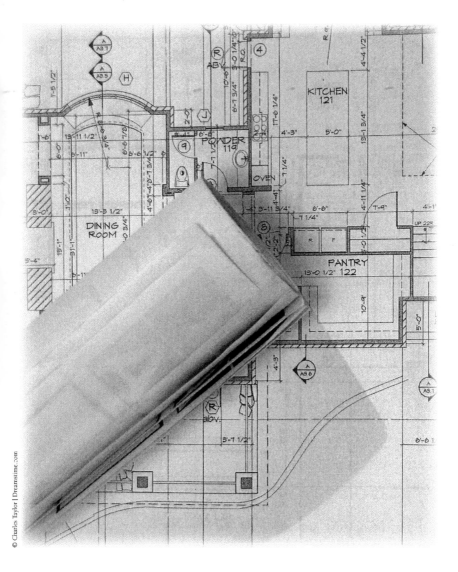

© Gordon Swanson | Dreamstime.com

Cultural Norms

*I*n our house of biblical interpretation, cultural norms are the decorating schemes we put together to accent our timeless truth walls, which are on top of the framework of our gospel of grace house. Cultural norms are the colors of paint we use, the pile of the carpets we install, the style of lights that we hang in our rooms. Cultural norms are personally satisfying. But as any interior decorator knows, one person's idea of a beautiful room can be downright ugly to someone else. In biblical interpretation, the verses that are put in the category of cultural norms may actually be timeless truths for other people. Some timeless truths may be another group's cultural norms.

In the Hebrew Testament, a huge selection of scripture helps define what it means to be a child of God in the Hebrew tradition. The custom of circumcising male children (Gen. 17:10–14); the practice of honoring God on the Sabbath (Lev. 22:3); observing prescribed festivals and holy days every year starting with the Passover (Lev. 23:4–5); observing the festival of weeks at the end of the wheat harvest (Lev. 23:15); celebrating the feasts of trumpets in the seventh lunar month (Lev. 23:23); celebrating the Day of Atonement (Lev. 23:26); fulfilling the festival of Tabernacles, which begins on the fifteenth day of the seventh month and lasts for seven days (Lev. 23:33); and placing a mezuzah on the doorposts of the tent or house (Deut. 11:20). These are but a sampling of the texts that help the children of Israel understand what it means to be part of the Jewish culture.

It is interesting to notice that even though all these verses are included in the Christian Bible, few of these texts would be considered timeless truths for Christian literalists or selectivists. Christians would consider most of these verses as prescribing cultural norms for Hebrew children of God. In contrast, all these verses might be considered timeless truths by people growing up in the Hebrew culture. For Christians these verses are historical, informative, and interesting, but not necessarily binding. I don't know of any Christian group that expects their members to literally practice all the verses above. That is not to say some verses from this corpus of material are not considered applicable to Christians. For example, there is a denomination of people who observe the biblical Sabbath (Seventh Day Adventists). These folks take Leviticus 22:3 to indicate the literal time for worship. In addition, I have heard countless sermons on the importance of tithing 10 percent of my income to

God's purposes (Deut. 14:22ff.). The tithe is considered a timeless truth by many literalists and selectivists in Christianity. Although Christian pastors often recommend their members tithe, in reality few Christians think it should apply literally to them. It seems everyone who chooses not to see a text as applying to himself or herself has just become a selectivist! How many folks are left who think they take every verse of the Bible literally?

Different groups of Christians debate the placement of many verses in the Greek Testament. Is it a timeless truth wall or a cultural norm color scheme? Here are some examples of texts that faithful people put in different categories. The celebration of the Lord's Supper (Eucharist, Holy Communion) is first prescribed in 1 Corinthians 11:23–26. The apostle Paul lets the church in Corinth and all subsequent readers know that the bread is Christ's body broken for humankind and the cup holds Christ's blood shed for the forgiveness of sins. Yes, Holy Communion is to be in remembrance of Christ's death and resurrection until he comes again. In many ways the celebration of Communion is a timeless truth that every Christian should observe. However, it becomes a cultural norm by how it is handled or what people believe happens to the elements. Some Christian traditions believe the bread and wine are transformed into the body and blood of Jesus (during a process called transubstantiation) and the words of institution can only be done by an ordained clergy person. Other Christians believe that the bread remains bread and the wine remains wine, but Jesus' spirit is mysteriously present (in a process called consubstantiation) and anyone can say the words of institution. Some Christian denominations use unleavened bread and wine while others use broken crackers and grape juice. The Bible doesn't prescribe what elements should be used. Over time, however, each religious group decided their cultural norm by the elements used and the frequency with which Communion is celebrated. The spectrum goes from those churches that believe Communion must be celebrated at every Mass to those that believe Communion should be celebrated a couple times a month to those who celebrate the Eucharist only quarterly. Whatever tradition you embrace your church has selected verses that support its particular practice.

A second text that receives a variety of interpretations is Acts 2:1–4. The text describes the arrival of the Holy Spirit among the disciples in Jerusalem. One of the outcomes of the Spirit's arrival that day was that the Galileans present were miraculously able to speak languages from around the world. For some denominations, the receiving of a foreign language from the baptism of the Spirit has become a timeless truth. To be fulfilled in the faith, they claim, everyone should receive a tangible gift of "tongues" from the Holy Spirit. Denominations that believe in the importance and power of the baptism of the Holy Spirit will turn to texts such as 1 Corinthians 14:5, which says, "I would like every one of you to speak in tongues," or Romans 8:26, which says, "In the same way, the Spirit helps us in our weakness. We do not know what we ought to pray for, but the Spirit himself intercedes for us with groans that words cannot express." If receiving and using "tongues" in prayer is a timeless truth for people, it will be a regular part of their life at home and even in corporate worship.

For other Christians, Acts 2 is not interpreted as a timeless truth that every believer should experience. Instead, they view "speaking in tongues" as a cultural norm. These selectivists would say that the Holy Spirit is free to touch people without giving them a foreign language that they did not learn. Some Christians believe that speaking in tongues was part of a special dispensation for the first century, but is no longer needed in the twenty-first century. Other Christians would suggest that speaking in an unlearned foreign language defines the culture of the Pentecostal traditions, but does not necessarily play a role in mainline churches. It should be obvious that individuals, congregations, and denominations do not all agree about whether to regard Acts 2 as a timeless truth or a cultural norm. It can be equally interpreted as a timeless truth to be universally expected or a cultural norm that applies only to those groups that incorporate it into their faith life. The real question becomes this: is Acts 2 a timeless truth wall for you or more like red paint put on as an expression of your cultural norm?

One other example, in Paul's letter to the young pastor, Timothy, the apostle describes some qualities desired for people who would be overseers in the early church. In 1 Timothy 3:2, Paul writes, "Now the overseer must be above reproach, the husband of but one wife . . ." This one quality is mentioned among eleven others. Over the years I have observed this text being used in numerous ways. In one denomination it is seen as a time-less truth, dictating that a pastor cannot divorce and remarry. If he did, he would be the husband of more than one wife. In another denomination this verse is seen as a cultural norm, implying that the pastor can only have one wife at a time. Obviously, this verse can be a timeless truth for any church that believes it is acceptable for pastors to be married! But for churches that hold that their ordained clergy must be single, this verse is considered a cultural norm. Same verse, diverse applications.

Cultural norms are characterized by being changeable, too. Just as a room can be repainted and recarpeted, so, too, can cultural norms be changed. In 2006 the Roman Catholic Church publicly acknowledged that it was considering rescinding its teaching about limbo (the incomplete afterlife postulated by the Roman Catholic Church in the Middle Ages for infants who die before being baptized). In the fifth century C.E., Augustine, the bishop of the city of Hippo in North Africa, declared that babies who died without baptismal grace would go to hell. That decree, although considered normative for hundreds of years, proved to be problematic and too harsh for theologians in the Middle Ages. The church leaders in the Middle Ages then proposed limbo as a place where children would go until they received the prayers and grace necessary to enter heaven. By the late 1500s, leaders of the Protestant reformation, men such as Martin Luther in Germany and John Calvin in Switzerland, had already rejected the idea of limbo. They postulated that God's grace would cover infants immediately upon their deaths. In 2006, nearly five hundred years later, the Roman Catholic Church was coming to a similar understanding.

I encourage you to notice that in the history of Christianity, many biblical texts have been moved from the timeless truth category to the cultural norm category and vice versa. However, regardless of what we are doing with these texts, the Bible's frame of grace is neither altered nor weakened. The repainting of internal walls or the recarpeting of internal hallways does not threaten the integrity of the gospel of grace foundation that holds the Bible together. We are free to move texts from one category to another as our experience or the Spirit of God leads us. Our house built upon the rock of grace will not fall down.

Exercise: If you would like to take a more comprehensive look at some Hebrew cultural texts, look up the following: Lev. 5; Lev. 6:1, 6:14, 6:24-30; Lev. 7:11; Num. 6:30; Num. 28.

For an informative look at some other texts whose status as timeless truth or cultural norm Christian groups debate, check out the following: Mark 16; John 15:12ff.; Eph. 4:1–16; Rev. 21:1–5; 22:7, 22:12, 22:13. Look up each text and ask yourself: Who is speaking? Who is being addressed? What is the message being communicated? Would you consider each verse a timeless truth for you or a cultural norm?

And here are some additional questions to ponder: Are there any Bible verses that you have moved from the timeless truth category to the cultural norm category? Are there any texts that you have given greater regard since an experience in your life? In 2000 Bruce Wilkinson singled out an obscure verse in the Hebrew Testament, 1 Chronicles 4:10, which says, "Jabez cried out to the God of Israel, 'Oh, that you would bless me and enlarge my territory! Let your hand be with me, and keep me from harm so that I will be free from pain.' and God granted his request." Wilkinson suggested this verse was a timeless truth and wrote a wonderfully successful book entitled *The Prayer of Jabez*. Many people found this book insightful and inspirational. Would you have considered the text a timeless truth before he wrote the book? Are there verses you have encountered that you think should be timeless truths? Are there timeless truth verses you would consider cultural norms? Write them down or mark them in the margin of your favorite reading or study Bible. You can begin to see which verses are timeless truths for you and which ones are cultural norms in your opinion. Now, as you consider encountering people who interpret the texts differently than you do, how might you have a conversation about the category into which you each put a verse?

© Gregory Henry | Dreamstime.com

*P*ersonal *O*pinions

*I*n our house of biblical interpretation, personal opinions are also considered part of the decorating scheme. Once the foundation of grace is established and its frame erected, the internal walls of timeless truth are in place and painted, and the basic carpeting and lighting put into place, the colors and fabrics and decorations we hang are subject to our personal tastes. The Bible presents readers with numerous verses that appear to be the opinion of the human author who wrote it. Let's look at some examples.

The Hebrew Testament includes a wisdom book called Ecclesiastes. Although scholars debate whether the book was written by King Solomon nine hundred years before Jesus or by a teacher named Queholeth in the second century BCE, the essence of the author's message revolves around his personal opinions. The early portion of the book details how the author, as he sought meaning and fulfillment, explored a number of different paths. Each attempt was met with success at first, and then he comes to the same conclusion, that "everything was meaningless, a chasing after the wind." (Eccles. 2:11, 2:15, 2:19, 2:21, 2:23, 2:26; 4:4, 4:8, 4:16; 5:10). Is everything in life really meaningless? No; the author does throw in a few verses that express hope. Check out Ecclesiastes 8:15 and 9:7–10. In these verses the teacher expresses his opinion about what makes life enjoyable. Look up what he has to say. Do you agree with his opinion?

Another text that captures an individual's feeling is Psalm 22:1. In the text the writer cries "My God, My God, why have you forsaken me?" Who hasn't had that feeling at some traumatic moment in life? The words suggest that God abandoned the writer. Do we really believe God abandons anyone? This verse might sound very familiar to any Christian who remembers the crucifixion account recorded in Matthew 27:47. In Matthew, Jesus hangs on the cross, dying, and he utters that exact verse as he feels the weight of the sins of the world bearing down on his body. Had God really abandoned Jesus? Or was Jesus expressing the same feeling that every human being does when life challenges seem to be crushing our spirit. Excruciating pain, feelings of abandonment, moments of desperate isolation always make us feel alone. Those feelings are all part of our personal experiences. Is God really gone at those times? Has God really abandoned us? I would have to say no; God is never gone nor has he abandoned us. However, the feeling of being alone is real and God's presence becomes more of a faith statement than a felt perception. The feeling of isolation does not negate God's presence. The feeling is personal and the opinion is that of the person in trauma.

The Greek Testament contains numerous verses that express the opinions of the authors. In 1 Corinthians 7, the apostle Paul makes very clear that he has some opinions for his readers in Corinth about marriage. He says, "To the rest I say this (I, not the Lord); If any brother has a wife who is not a believer and she is willing to live with him, he must not divorce her." Please note the parenthetical words: Paul is making it quite clear that this is his personal opinion and not a command from God. Then a few verses later he reiterates his personal biases about unmarried folks. He continues, "Now about virgins: I have no command from the Lord, but I give a judgment as one who by the Lord's mercy is trustworthy." He goes on to suggest that, given the urgency of the situation (expecting Jesus' return at any time), it was better for people to stay in the relational status in which they already found themselves. If single, stay single. If married, stay married. Regardless of their situation, Paul was crystal clear in saying that the verses of advice that were about to follow were his opinion and not a direct command from God.

In Paul's letter to Timothy, the elder apostle instructs his young protégé to take better physical care of himself. Paul advises, "Stop drinking only water, and use a little wine because of your stomach and frequent illnesses" (1 Tim. 5:23). For all those conservative Christian denominations that prohibit the use of any alcohol, this text is never preached as a timeless truth! Rather, for them and for members of Alcoholics Anonymous, the suggested libation is surely the personal opinion of the apostle, one that merely suggests that Timothy take a commonly held first-century home remedy for his stomach problems. In some conservative circles this would not be a truth to be passed on to all future generations.

If we view such biblical passages as expressing personal opinions, how are we to treat them? We are free to place them in our house of interpretation as we see fit or feel led by the Holy Spirit. Some Christian churches have taken the text about a church leader's marital status and made it a timeless truth. In so doing, they prohibit their clergy from marrying. If it is considered a timeless truth it is to be lived out in real life, and you can only admire the fact that they follow their interpretation.

In other cases, personal opinions can be informative but not deemed as instructions to be followed by everyone and for all time. Everyone with a stomach problem is not expected to use wine to treat the ailment! If the texts are perceived as an author's personal opinion, they will not have a binding influence on future generations. Paul gave advice on a spectrum of subjects. Here are some examples. Consider his advice about hair length. If we understand that it is Paul's personal opinion that men should have short hair and women long hair (1 Cor. 11:14–16), then men and women in other generations can wear their hair any length they want. If Paul's advice that women stay silent in congregations (1 Cor. 14:34) is interpreted as his personal opinion for the church in Corinth, then women today can speak freely, hold offices in a church, and even serve as ordained clergy. If Paul's thoughts about resolving conflicts among Christians without the use of the legal court system (1 Cor. 6) are his opinion for the first-century church, then there may be reason for the legal court system to be used in future generations. Personal opinions that have been included in scripture can be considered the colors and fabrics that decorate our biblical interpretation house. Yes, we can hang different pictures on the walls, put down new throw rugs, and hang new shades on the lights. The house will look and feel different, but the house of biblical interpretation will not fall down.

Exercise: If you would like to do more research into personal opinions in the Bible, look up the following texts: Job 4:1–8; 8:1–4; 20:1–8; Prov. 14:1; 1 Cor. 7:17–24; 16:1–3; 2 Cor. 6:14–18; 8:8–12; Acts 15:36–41;

Col. 3:18–25; 1 Tim. 5:9–15. Once you read them, determine the following: Who is speaking? What is the subject being addressed? Is the advice being offered a timeless truth, a cultural norm, or a personal opinion?

And here are some additional questions to ponder: have you had anyone give you his or her personal opinion and then realize that the person expected you to treat it as a timeless truth? Have you ever had a person give you his or her timeless truth only to assign it to the personal opinion category? Why do you think some of Paul's texts have become timeless truths, even though in Paul's writing he specifically says his directives should not be considered a word from the Lord? What do you think prompts people to do what the words on the page say not to do?

Chris Kodenberg | Dreamstime.com

Random,
Unusual Texts

*T*he house of biblical interpretation contains some verses that resemble an ugly lamp you may have inherited from your grandmother many years ago. The lamp does not fit in the decor of your home. What to do with it? In essence, some verses just don't seem to fit into any message the Bible seems to communicate.

In the Hebrew Testament there is an amazing story about the ninth-century BCE prophet Elisha. When traveling toward the village of Bethel, a gang of teenage boys verbally harasses him. The boys publicly ridicule his baldness. Then the story takes a macabre turn. In an inexplicable act of revenge Elisha turns and in the Lord's name curses the young hooligans. The result is astonishing: "Then two bears came out of the woods and mauled forty-two of the youths." (2 Kings 2:24). What does this story tell us about the gospel of God's acceptance, forgiveness, and grace? Nothing! Is this a timeless truth? If so, would it be that as a prophet of God you can curse those who offend you and wild animals will wreak havoc on your enemy? This is probably not a timeless truth. It does not qualify as a cultural norm either, as we see no other examples of such revenge anywhere in scripture. Is this the personal opinion of the writer of 2 Kings? If this is a description of a literal event in history what category does it fit in? If this is a selective teaching story, what is the message to be taken from it? This story does not seem to fit in any category other than a random unusual text. I have never heard a sermon on this text, nor is it ever included in church lectionary readings. I am not sure any Sunday school or vacation Bible school curriculum would want to include it in their lessons either. One can only imagine the terror young children might feel if they thought wild animals could come screaming out of the woods and maul children at a religious leader's command. Why is this story in the Bible? I really do not know.

Another Hebrew Testament text creates some interesting imagery. In Genesis 6 we encounter a race of supernatural men called Nephilim who choose to come to earth and marry daughters of human beings. The couples conceive children who become "heroes of old, men of renown" (Gen. 6:4). These children are referenced later in the Hebrew Testament in books such as 2 Samuel 21 and 1 Chronicles 20. The thought of sons of God taking human brides and creating a race of giants has a great deal of appeal. In a modern world that loves action heroes like Superman, Spiderman, and the Bionic Woman, it would seem the Bible has some characters ready to be discovered. Yet, none of the Nephilim ever get mentioned in faith stories. Other than the giant Goliath who young David pummels in the Valley of Elah, giants play no major role in the Bible. Could we live without this unusual text? Yes, I think so. It really does not teach us anything about grace. It gives us no insights on living a life of faith nor does it help us understand any cultural or personal opinions. Why is it still in the Bible? Only God knows.

In 2 Samuel we find a very gruesome story about rape, a contract killing, and intrigue in a royal family. This could qualify as a script for a television program. The biblical story certainly has all the ingredients for a current event. In chapter 13 we read about the brutal rape of David's daughter, Tamar, by her half brother Amnon. It is the only rape recorded in the Bible. After Tamar has been disgraced, her brother Absalom puts out a contract to have her attacker killed. Two years later the contract is fulfilled: Amnon is murdered. The sister is avenged. The story concludes with Tamar as a desolate woman, her half brother dead, her avenging brother on the run and her father mourning the death of her half brother. This story certainly carries the elements of a real tragedy. Is there any message about grace to be found? Is there a timeless truth to be uncovered? Is revenge something families should seek on their own? To each question I perceive the answer to be no. This text does affirm the fallenness of human beings and the desolation that violence bestows on all who experience and employ it. However, could we live without this text in the Bible? I think so.

One of the more unusual practices prescribed in the Bible is found in Deuteronomy 25:5–6. Here we learn that it is imperative for a brother to marry his deceased brother's widow. The text says, "Her husband's brother shall take her and marry her and fulfill the duty of a brother-in-law to her. The first son she bears shall carry on the name of the dead brother so that his name will not be blotted out from Israel." If this verse were considered a timeless truth and the surviving brother were already married, the Bible would endorse polygamy! If it is perceived as only a cultural norm applying to unmarried living brothers and benefiting a childless family in the ancient Hebrew nation, then it has no bearing on the modern world. According to the Bible, if the living brother did not want to marry his brother's widow, the widow was given permission to complain to the city elders. If the brother-in-law persisted in refusing the marriage, the city elders were instructed to go as a group and confront him about his lack of respect for his brother's family. If the living brother continued to refuse his matrimonial duty, the widow was permitted to humiliate him in public. In addition, the living brother's family would be given a derogatory name. Read Deuteronomy 25:7–10 to learn of the entire prescription.

These verses are certainly not claimed as literal timeless truths in today's Christian world. Most selectivists would call these verses cultural norms aimed at meeting the perceived need of the ancient Hebrew world and its concern that eternal life be rendered through a father's male offspring. Notice that in the Deuteronomy text, no mention is given that the sexual encounter between the brother and his sister-in-law is adultery. No mention is made that the living brother's first wife can object to this new woman in her home. What is also intriguing is that this verse is a direct contradiction to what the Bible says in Leviticus 20:21. Here, the Bible says, "If a man marries his brother's wife, it is an act of impurity; he has dishonored his brother. They will be childless." Interesting, isn't it? If a man's brother is alive, marrying a sister-in-law dishonors the family and, as a consequence of disobeying the ordinance, the new couple will be childless. However, if a married brother dies, the rules change. The surviving brother is expected to marry his sister-in-law and they honor the deceased brother by bearing a male child. This ruling may seem confusing, but it makes sense if your only means of living in the future is through your name being carried on by your male offspring. As you can see, within the Bible itself, the rules can and do change. What is considered a sin in Leviticus is an obligation in Deuteronomy. Circumstances themselves change how the act is viewed. Might this foreshadow how the Bible's verses can reinterpret one another? What is considered a timeless truth in one situation becomes a less binding cultural norm or personal opinion in another situation. What do you think?

Random unusual texts are not limited to the Hebrew Testament. The Greek Testament contains some very perplexing passages. One of the most challenging is found in chapter 5 of Acts. Luke tells the story in the context of the relationships between families in the early church in Jerusalem. In the text, two members of the congregation, Ananias and Sapphira, sell a piece of property they own together. The expectation among the followers of Jesus at the time was that members who sold anything shared their earned profits with the group. Nothing was to be held back. The ethos was all for one, one for all. Obviously, human nature is susceptible to the temptation of selfishness. Well, selfish is just what Ananias and Sapphira turn out to be. They sold their land, and in an effort to keep more of the proceeds for themselves, they agreed to lie to Peter about the amount of money they received for their property. They created a plan and executed it perfectly. However, they were not prepared for the consequences. Ananias brought the smaller amount of money to Peter and then willingly lied, saying he had given all they had received. The text does not say how Peter knew Ananias was lying, but Peter immediately verbally chastises Ananias. "When Ananias heard this, he fell down and died" (Acts 5:5).

The text does not say what caused the death. All we know is that Ananias dies and this is where the story begins to become difficult to interpret. Fear grips the followers and some young men from the congregation immediately bury Ananias. To be buried quickly was not unusual, but the lack of pastoral care that follows is dumbfounding.

Peter and the other disciples appear to make no effort to tell Sapphira that her husband has died. Neither do they express any empathy for her loss nor sympathy for the unexpected death. In fact, Peter makes no consoling comments whatsoever. In what appears to be a cold and calculating manner, Peter, upon seeing Sapphira, asks if the discounted price is in fact the full price they had received for the property. An unsuspecting Sapphira willingly lies and corroborates the story she and her husband, had conspired to use. Then Peter chastises her for lying and coldly tells her that the pall bearers are just returning from burying her husband and she will be joining him. "At that moment she fell down at his feet and died" (Acts 5:10).

Is there any message about grace to be gleaned from this story? I don't see it. If this were a text to be included as a timeless truth, every financial stewardship campaign would become a time of terror and grief for unsuspecting church members everywhere! Peter would never have passed clinical pastoral education for his confrontational handling of Ananias and his uncompassionate handling of Sapphira. This text certainly gives us insights on the interdependence of the early church culture, but it gives no parameter about how followers of Jesus are to treat one another. Be honest or else! Probably not. Many scholars see this text as a first-century retelling of the story found in Joshua 7. In the ancient story, Achan, a Hebrew army officer, steals spoils from the conquest of Jericho. When it is discovered that Achan first stole the items and then lied to Joshua about it, Achan was tried and convicted and stoned to death by the people of Israel according to the law of the time. Again, there is no grace to be found in this story. Some might see the reality of severe consequences for lying to God, but no one literally gets stoned to death for such dishonesty today. What purposes do these texts serve? You will have to discern for yourself.

Another Greek Testament text is found in the apostle Paul's second letter to the church in Corinth. Paul reveals to his readers a vision that he had years before. Two Corinthians 12 starts with this: "I must go on boasting. Although there is nothing to be gained, I will go on to visions and revelations from the Lord. I know a man in Christ who fourteen years ago was caught up to the third heaven." Third heaven? Since when does Christianity teach that there are levels of heaven? According to this text Paul is describing just such an arrangement. If this text were perceived as a literalist timeless truth then there would be at least three levels of heaven and each would have to be given a name and reason for being. If this text is perceived as a selectivist cultural norm, we might understand that first-century Judaism had a perception that heaven was tiered. If this is Paul's personal opinion based on his vision or a friend's experience on a particular day fourteen years before writing the letter, then it would not be a view that all Christians should have to accept forever. I see it as a random text. As such, it presents a unique image of life after death with no supporting information. As you can see, this text might be placed in several of the category possibilities we have discussed. Where would you choose to put it?

In the Greek Testament we encounter these words: "But do not forget this one thing, dear friends: with the Lord a day is like a thousand years, and a thousand years are like a day" (2 Pet. 3:8). What implications would this have for the Genesis 1 text we talked about earlier? If this text is taken as a literalist timeless truth, then the creation story could actually have taken six twenty-four hour days or six thousand years with the last thousand years for rest! If this text is taken as a selectivist timeless truth, its message might be that the way humans measure time is not God's measurement. Our prayers may be answered immediately in God's perception, but in human terms it may take a long time for the answer to manifest. If this verse is just Peter's personal opinion, then there may not be a need to measure God's timing in human terms. Once again, this text can be put in different categories. Which one would you choose?

This is not meant to be an exhaustive listing of all unusual passages in scripture. For most people, these stories are totally unknown. However, the fact that these verses have each been in the Bible for thousands of years suggests they cannot just be ignored; they must be considered. What are we to do with them? As I have already suggested, their value is questionable. They may very well serve a purpose in someone's mind, but I struggle with the value they bring to my understanding of faith and life. Like furniture that doesn't really fit the decor of a newly constructed house, these passages do not add much to my house of biblical interpretation. Were these texts to be deleted from the Bible, our house of biblical interpretation would not collapse, nor would it become less attractive. In fact, I would speculate, most of us have lived in our biblical house without even knowing these verses were present. Certainly our houses would not be dramatically altered if they were gone.

There is one more category of random texts that I would like to briefly address. There are passages of scripture that communicate diametrically opposing messages. These passages are seldom seen together. When I see them side by side, I wonder which side of the message we are to make timeless truths and which side of the argument are cultural norms. Are these verses walls or basic color schemes? I do not believe any of them represent the foundational gospel of grace. Therefore, their presence does not make the house stronger nor does their absence threaten the demise of the house. Let's look at a couple of these texts.

In Exodus 20:13 we read "You shall not murder." This is one of the original ten commandments that Moses receives from God on Mount Sinai. This would seem to be an easy timeless truth for literalists and selectivists alike. However, scripture gets complicated in the next chapter. Exodus 21:12 informs us, "Anyone who strikes a man and kills him shall surely be put to death." It is the stated consequence of killing another person that the person who killed be killed in turn. Should this apply to the executioner as well? Apparently not. The early codes also called for the death penalty to be applied to belligerent children (Lev. 20:9), adulterous men and women (Lev. 20:10), and incestuous relatives (Lev. 20:11–12). The list goes on and on. How does the timeless truth "you shall not murder" fit with a penal system based on executing the offenders? If that question were not challenging enough we have internal examples from the Hebrew and Greek Testaments that conflict.

Let's consider what happens to the first recorded murderer. In Genesis 4, Cain kills his brother, Abel, in an act of jealous rage. When God discovers Cain's murder, is Cain's punishment execution? No, Cain is punished by being cursed. He has to work the land and be a restless wanderer. Cain's response is predictably an ancient version of poor me: "My punishment is more than I can bear . . . I will be a restless wanderer on the earth, and whoever finds me will kill me" (Gen. 4:13–14). God responds, "Then the Lord put a mark on Cain so that no one who found him would kill him" (Gen. 4:15). God's response was not to execute him but rather give him grace in the form of a mark that protected him from being murdered. Granted, in Genesis the law is not technically in affect yet. But isn't it interesting that God does not practice here what might be considered God's law later, namely the execution of murderers? In fact, after the law is in effect all those guilty of murder are still not executed. In Deuteronomy 19 we learn that there were to be cities of refuge created to house those who were guilty of murder but did not deserve the death penalty. Is the penalty for murder death or not? Achan was executed according to the law. In Cain's case the law was not applied. Which is right? The answer is a mixed message!

The Greek Testament also presents us with an example of the inconsistency with which God's law was applied in the Bible itself.

In John 8 we are told that the Pharisees brought to Jesus a woman who was caught in the act of adultery. It is interesting to note that they only brought the woman; it seems that the man involved was not going to be held accountable as Leviticus 20:10 required. When Jesus was presented with the scenario he writes in the dirt and then recommends that the person who had no sin throw the first stone. (Stoning was the prescribed method of execution for adultery and the practice was that the people who bore witness in the case throw the first stones.) When the crowd dissipates without any stones being hurled, Jesus pronounces grace on the woman, and she is allowed to leave not only alive but also forgiven. If Jesus, God's Son, does not keep the requirements of the law regarding the death penalty, how should we understand the biblical requirement of the death penalty?

Both literalists and selectivists are faced with a quandary. Which of these texts are to be taken literally and which are to be taken figuratively? Who decides? In Cain's case, God chose to deviate from his own later command. In Deuteronomy someone had to decide if the murderer was to be punished by death or sent to the city of refuge. In the first century, the Pharisees made the decision to not execute the man, and Jesus made the decision that the letter of the law could be reinterpreted for the woman as well. Is the message in our modern world that we, too, are allowed to decide when the letter of the law is to be followed and when the letter of the law can be altered? If the law says the penalty for murder is death and this law is a timeless truth, it should be followed. If it is a cultural norm, it is open to interpretation. The Bible itself presents us with conflicting examples. How will you decide?

Exercises: Here are some examples that present more opportunities for studying some mixed messages found in the Bible. I recommend reading each of the following texts: Lev. 20:21, Deut. 25:5–6, Lev. 20:25, and Matt. 15:10–11. Then discern your own answers to the following: Who is the audience? What is the issue? What does the law require? Is the law altered? If so, by whom? If not, why not? Is this law a timeless truth for you or a cultural norm?

Here are some additional questions to consider: Are there other Bible verses that seem to present opposing views of the same subject? How do you decide which one you will make a timeless truth and which one will be a cultural norm? How do you handle people who put those verses in different categories than you do?

Dri | Dreamstine.com

Putting *the* Tools *to* Work

Our house of biblical interpretation is finally built. The framework of the gospel of grace is secure. Our internal walls of timeless truths have been designed to give us the space we need. The cultural norms and personal opinions have decorated each of the rooms, and we know we have random texts that are awkwardly stored in our house. Now, what do we do when reading and studying the

Bible? We can begin using the house to help us understand our reading and study of the Bible.

I have encouraged students over the years to read the Bible and mark in the margins whether a particular verse, chapter, or pericope (a completed story or thought that transcends chapters) is a G2 (gospel of grace), a T2 (timeless truth), a CN (cultural norm), a PO (personal opinion), or a RT (random text). When folks reread chapters and verses weeks, months, or years later they are able to see if their perception of the text's appropriate category has remained the same or has changed. If it has changed, I encourage identifying the circumstances or Spirit-driven insights that caused the change. Let's take a look at several case studies demonstrating how the house of biblical interpretation works in the real world of Christian living.

Case Study Insight: **Role of Tension in the Bible**

During my college years, a Simon and Garfunkel album inspired me to pick and pluck my way through their songs. When my first guitar string broke I had to learn how to replace it. I discovered that my guitar would only make music if there was the proper tension on each of the strings. The nut on one end of the string and the peg on the other enabled me to adjust the tension so that all six strings were in the right balance. When the tension was right, I could eventually (with practice) play decent music. The need for tension is behind every stringed instrument: piano, banjo, harp, violin, cello, etc. The music is only possible when each string is tuned to the proper tension. This same principle began to make sense for me when it came to interpreting the Bible as well.

God has allowed a certain amount of tension in the Bible so that the music of salvation can be played. Over the course of history, texts that conflict have not necessarily been weeded out because the Bible is really a library of books about faith. It is not a science book, it is not a math book, and it is not a history book. It is a relational library. It records God's relationship with creation. And it makes observations about the relationships between creatures and the creator as well. God does not ask people to check their minds at the door when they enter the realm of biblical understanding and biblical "house-building." Rather, God empowers us to live with this library, to talk about the library, and to pray for wisdom as we study the library. God sends the Spirit to direct us. In John's Gospel Jesus tells his followers that the Spirit will lead the way to understanding. He says, "But when he, the Spirit of truth, comes, he will guide you into all truth" (John 16:13). This is a timeless truth I believe in deeply. If the Spirit leads us to different understandings, then let's live together agreeing to disagree.

Case Study One: Life Experiences Remodel the House

During my first seminary experience my practical education site was in a Baptist church. One of the families I got to know had expressed very strong feelings that divorce was a sin. For them Matthew 19:3–6 was a timeless truth. "Therefore, what God has joined together, let man not separate" (19:6b). In their minds there were no exceptions to be considered. In fact, there were several incidences I heard about where they as a couple had put their timeless truths to work. According to their understanding of Matthew 18:15 they felt that they were obligated to go to their brothers and sisters and share their concern. So that is exactly what they did. They informed their fellow members that being separated was only acceptable if they were choosing to pray (1 Cor. 7:5) and that under no circumstance should they consider divorce. At the time I was impressed with how the family both knew and implemented the verses they had decided were timeless truths.

I finished seminary and went on to work at a different church across town. Several years later I ran into the couple in a shopping mall. They were very gracious, filling me in on the news about their life and family. However, I was startled to hear them say that their oldest daughter had just gotten remarried. Remembering their hard-line stance on divorce I cautiously asked them how they felt about that. I was not prepared for their response. Well, in their minds, their daughter's experience was "different." It seems her ex-husband turned out to be abusive to their daughter. Her new husband was a wonderful Christian man and all seemed well. They had recently discovered Deuteronomy 24:2, which says, "And when she is departed out of his house, she may go and be another man's wife" (King James Version). They agreed. Given their understanding of their daughter's unique circumstance the Matthew 19 text no longer served as a binding timeless truth. Instead, it became a cultural norm that could be seen as not necessarily binding, regardless of circumstances. The new view of Deuteronomy 24:2 enabled them to perceive that divorce and remarriage were acceptable possibilities at least in their case.
The family had done some remodeling of their house of biblical interpretation. Life experiences had caused them to remodel their interpretations of several verses but the overall house had stood firm. How would you have responded to their news?

Case Study Two: **Opposite Strands in the House**

Certain factors we have not yet considered can influence the category in which we might place Bible passages. There are two conflicting strands found throughout the Hebrew and Greek Testaments. They are found in different writers at different times. In the house of biblical interpretation these strands are like the electrical wires that run throughout the walls of the house bringing electricity to all the rooms. The wires in the house are often color coded, red for hot wire, black for grounding wire, etc. The wires are not the same. They serve totally different purposes. In fact, they serve opposite ends. Yet, both are present. There are some distinctly different lines of thinking that go side by side in the Bible. We often don't see how they are connected or related to one another, but they are present nonetheless. They serve a very important function as each presents human thinking that has an impact on how we interpret the Bible.

The first strand is called deuteronomist or what I prefer to call old school thinking. The premise behind old school thought can be summarized as having two components. The first is this: if you obey God . . . God will reward you. There are numerous texts that literally reinforce this notion. Consider these: "Now if you obey me fully and keep my covenant, then out of all nations you will be my treasured possession" (Exod. 19:5); "Honor your father and mother, so that you may live long in the land the Lord your God is giving you" (Exod. 20:12); "Do what is right and good in the Lord's sight, so that it may go well with you and you may go in and take over the good land that the Lord promised on oath to your forefathers" (Deut. 6:18); and "Be careful to follow every command I am giving you today, so that you may live and increase and may enter and possess the land that the Lord promised on oath to your forefathers" (Deut. 8:1).

The second half of old school thought—succinctly put as claiming, "If you disobey God . . . God will punish you"— is also well documented. Consider these passages: "If you ever forget the Lord your God and follow other gods and worship and bow down to them, I testify against you today that you will surely be destroyed" (Deut. 8:19); and "See, I am setting before you a blessing and a curse—the blessing if you obey the commands of the Lord your God that I am giving you today; the curse if you disobey the command of the Lord your God and turn from the way that I command you today by following other gods, which you have not known" (Deut. 11:26–28).

If you obey God you will be rewarded. If you disobey God you will be punished. The old school thought is a part of the wiring of almost every house of biblical interpretation. Where and how do we experience it today?

Have you ever had something bad happen to you? Did the thought ever cross your mind, "God, why are you doing this to me?" or "Why are you letting this happen to me?" That is old school wiring at work. Have you ever told someone going through a tough time, "The Lord will never give you more than you can handle"? Then you were espousing old school logic. After all, it is apparently God who dispenses the challenges we must overcome. Old school logic is what the friends of Job were reciting when they sought to explain why Job's life was falling apart. Bildad tells Job, "When your children sinned against him, he gave them over to the penalty of their sin" (Job 8:4). Bildad's message is simple: Job, your children sinned and God punished them with death. Obviously, they had not obeyed God and that is why they died. Job's second neighbor, Zophar, tells his suffering acquaintance, "If you put away the sin that is in your hand and allow no evil to dwell in your tent, then you will lift up your face without shame" (Job 11:14–15a). In other words, his message is this: Job you have obviously sinned and when you confess the sin and get rid of the evil in your life then God's grace will be there for you and you will be free of shame. Another neighbor, Eliphaz, critically attacks Job for daring to claim there was no sin in his life that caused the calamities. Eliphaz says, "Your sin prompts your mouth; you adopt the tongue of the crafty; your own mouth condemns you not mine; your own lips testify against you" (Job 15:5–6). It was common knowledge among old school thinkers that if life was going well . . . God was blessing the person. If life was falling apart . . . obviously God must be punishing the person. The old school logic was not just a Hebrew Testament experience. It was present in Jesus' time as well.

In John 9 we find the story of Jesus and the disciples coming upon the man who had been born blind. The disciples asked the logical old school question: "Rabbi, who sinned, this man or his parents, that he was born blind?" (John 9:2). Obviously, blindness was a bad consequence. Someone had to have sinned in order for God to cause it to happen to this man. In the old school line of thinking all disasters, tragedies, illnesses, business setbacks, and crumbling relationships can be interpreted as a consequence of some sin in a person's, family's or a society's life.

Old school thinking is not only an approach practiced in biblical times; it is practiced in our world today. On more than one occasion I have heard some conservative Christian teachers say they believed the physical disease of AIDS was God's punishment on homosexuals; I have heard other conservative Christian speakers suggest the 9/11 attack on the Trade Centers in New York was God's punishment on a country that was no longer obeying God. Recently I have also read twenty-first century authors promise that if we obey God's commands we will experience health, wealth, and well being beyond our wildest dreams. All of these are examples of old school logic at work in the modern house of biblical interpretation. If you obey God you are rewarded . . . if you disobey God you will be punished. If a person erects these verses as timeless truth walls, then he or she will interpret the world in light of these truths. Good will be regarded as a reward and trouble will be interpreted as punishment from God.

Running alongside the old school line of thinking is a completely opposite approach. It is also found in the Hebrew and Greek Testaments. This counter logic is called non-deuteronomist, or as I prefer to call it, realist thinking. The realist view suggests that life is lived. Good and bad things happen to everyone. The world is an imperfect place with imperfect people making decisions with imperfect information. Life happens and good and bad can occur without them either being a blessing or a curse from God. The Hebrew Testament book of Ecclesiastes has a powerful summary of the realist view when it says, "Again I saw that under the sun the race is not always to the swift, nor the battle to the strong, nor bread to the wise, nor riches to the intelligent, nor favor to the skilled. But time and chance happen to them all" (Eccles. 9:11). The writer of Ecclesiastes was a realist who saw life both good and bad happening to all kinds of people.

The writer of Job appears to have been a realist as well, despite the old school thinking that the book also presents. Throughout the book Job doggedly refuses to admit the calamities that are transpiring are the result of his sin. He says, for example, "Then I would still have this consolation—my joy in unrelenting pain—that I had not denied the words of the Holy One" (Job 6:10). Job refuses his neighbors' old school explanations. Instead, Job recognizes the bad things that were happening to him as random acts and not as a result of God's punishment.

Realist thinking appears to be how Jesus chose to respond to the disciples in the John 9:3 text mentioned earlier: "Neither this man nor his parents sinned, Jesus said." Jesus did not see the old school logic as the explanation for the man's blindness. Instead, it was an opportunity for God to do something miraculous. Jesus is recorded in Matthew 5:45 as saying, "For he makes his sun rise on the evil and the good, and sends his rain on the righteous and the unrighteous." The realist view would interpret droughts, hurricanes, volcanic eruptions, and crop failures are the result of climatic or geological conditions, not God's punishment. The realist view would also suggest that buildings attacked by terrorists are not God's doing at all, but the result of imperfect people making deadly imperfect decisions. Realists would frequently interpret the escalating value of stocks, housing values, and personal fortunes as the result of bull-market conditions and good business practices, not necessarily God's reward. After all, there are fortunes made through illicit and illegal means as well.

We can pursue the contrast between strands further. As Christians we believe Jesus lived a life obedient to God's will. In most Christian circles, his life is believed to have been in perfect obedience to God's desires. If we measure his life in the old school logic, did Jesus receive wealth, accolades, and long life? No. It seems that his reward was being loved by some, respected by many, used by the needy, suspected by the powerful, rejected by the governing, hated by a few, and falsely accused, beaten, crucified, and eventually abandoned by nearly everyone. Old school logic would be forced to ask this: What sin did Jesus commit to receive such harsh punishment? Realists would say… that is what can happen to those who do good but are misinterpreted and mistreated by the people in power.

Another example would be the apostle Paul. He was obedient to his call to follow Jesus and make disciples in "Jerusalem, Judea, Samaria, and the uttermost parts of the earth" (Acts 1:8). Again, if we were to use old school logic, we would have to ask this question: was his faithfulness rewarded by wealth, health, and good fortune? According to Paul, "I have worked much harder, been in prison more frequently, been flogged more severely, and been exposed to death again and again" (2 Cor. 11:23). This is not exactly the reward of obedience the old school might suggest. In contrast, it is the realist view that, like Job, Paul was faithful to God and Paul felt God was faithful to him, even though life was difficult! If the Realist verses are perceived as timeless truth walls, then good and bad can and will happen to good and bad people alike. That is how life will be regarded in those houses of interpretation.

There is one other Greek Testament example of the confrontation between the old school and realist viewpoints that I would like to address. In Mark 1:17-25 we read the story of the young ruler who comes to Jesus and asks, "Good teacher, what must I do to inherit eternal life?" Jesus proceeds to ask him if he has obeyed all the commandments of God and the young man boldly proclaims, "Teacher . . . all these I have kept since I was a boy." Clearly this was an impressive young man. He had obeyed God and in old school logic he felt that he should have been rewarded with God's blessings. Indeed he was. In verse 22 we learn that the young man was very wealthy. To all the disciples watching this encounter, the young man was the poster child of old school logic: he had obeyed God his whole life and God rewarded him with wealth in this world. Surely this young man would be rewarded for his faithfulness with the ultimate gift of eternal life, too.

It is at this moment that Jesus seems to purposely shock the old school thinkers around him. Jesus asks, "How hard it is for the rich to enter the kingdom of God?" What? This was an incredible question, with incredible implications. It flew in the face of what every old school thinker accepted as the timeless truths of the Hebrew Testament, namely if you obey God you are rewarded in this life and surely in the next life as well. The disciples were stunned. Jesus then appears to make sure his realist point of view gets across when he adds, "It is easier for a camel to go through the eye of a needle than for a rich man to enter the kingdom of God." I do not believe this story is a statement about wealth. I believe it was Jesus attacking the old school view that wealth was always God's reward. Why was Jesus attacking old school logic? Because it did not describe his reality. As we already mentioned, Jesus' life of obedience did not bring him wealth, ease, or long life. Instead, his life of obedience was one of humble service to others. The byproducts of his service were pain and suffering, not material reward. Jesus was affirming that the realist view was how he was experiencing life.

This raises a question for each and every one of us: Which strand best defines how we understand the world? If we make the old school texts our timeless truths then we will view our successes as rewards from God and our failures as God's punishment. If we make the realist texts our timeless truths, then we will see that life can be either good or difficult, and that the circumstances of the world are not the result of God dispensing rewards or punishments. According to the realist, we do not have to take time trying to attach spiritual meaning to each and every event that befalls us. We can know good and bad happen to everyone. We do not have to question why God is doing this or that bad thing to us. Instead, we can celebrate God's presence sustaining us through all of life's events. This realist interpretation may appeal to you. In the end, every reader of the Bible will have to decide which line of thinking will be a timeless truth.

Case Study Three:
Scripture Remodeling Scripture about Sabbath

There are numerous occasions when one verse in the Bible is used to reinterpret another verse. A classic example is the observance of the day of rest. In Genesis 2 the seventh day arrives after God has finished the work he set out to do. On this day, he rested. The text reads, "And God blessed the seventh day and made it holy, because on it he rested from all the work of creating that he had done." Sabbath was started and made holy as a day of rest.

Nine hundred years before Jesus' life, honoring the Sabbath was one of the Ten Commandments Moses brought down from Mount Sinai. Exodus 20: 8–10 records the simple command to make it a day of rest violated by "neither you, nor your son or daughter, nor your manservant or maidservant, nor your animals, nor the alien within your gates." Religious people, non-religious people, Jews, Gentiles, humans, and animals all were to be given time to rest. Over time, however, resting was not regarded as an adequate way to keep the Sabbath holy.

During the seventh century BCE the people of Israel were in captivity.

Observing the Sabbath was more difficult as their foreign masters did not necessarily give them time off from their labor. Sunset on Friday became the beginning time for Sabbath. In Deuteronomy 5 we read a new rendering of the Ten Commandments, these written three hundred years later than the Exodus version. In the Deuteronomy text the people of Israel are reminded of their first captivity in Egypt. They are reminded that God eventually rescued them, an encouraging reminder for people in a time of bondage. As time goes on and circumstances change, keeping the Sabbath holy became more challenging. In Numbers 28:9 we are told that offerings are to be made on the Sabbath, something that had become part of making the day holy. People knew to do no work, but other questions began to arise. What constitutes work? The answer wasn't obvious, For example, if a farmer's only cow falls in a ditch, is it work to pull it out? If the farmer were to leave it there, surely the cow would die and with it, so would part of the farmer's livelihood. These questions and others like them led to the development of codes of conduct that prescribed acceptable and unacceptable behavior on the Sabbath.

By the time Jesus began ministering in Israel the rules detailing how to observe the Sabbath were complex and encompassing. In Matthew 12 we learn that the disciples and Jesus created a disturbance because they did not follow all the "fine print" in keeping the Sabbath holy. Finally, Jesus confronts the keepers of the law, saying, "The Sabbath was made for man, not man for the Sabbath." (Mark 2:27). In other words, Jesus reinterpreted the teachers of the law's accepted understanding of scriptures. The religious leaders had heard and passed on for centuries the regulations about not working on the Sabbath. Now Jesus was introducing a new understanding of their Bible. Humans were not created just to conform to all the rules, Jesus suggested. Instead, Sabbath was made so that people could rest and honor God. According to Jesus, returning to the Genesis approach of keeping the Sabbath holy was not about fulfilling the thirty-nine rules that had accumulated over time. Rather, it was about honoring God. Jesus would go on to honor God by healing on the Sabbath, forgiving sins on the Sabbath, feeding people on the Sabbath, and teaching on the Sabbath, and in so doing, he told the rule watchers of his day that honoring God was how the Sabbath was to be spent. This was a radical departure from the accepted first-century understanding. Jesus' seemingly cavalier actions on the Sabbath would contribute to getting him in trouble with the religious establishment.

In the Jewish world the Sabbath was and still begins at sundown Friday and lasts until sundown on Saturday. In most Christian communities, however, Sabbath is no longer considered to be Friday. Instead, most Christians celebrate the day Jesus arose from the dead, so Sunday became the day to honor God. Honoring God on the historic Sabbath, Friday, is no longer considered a timeless truth. In its place a new Sabbath was created as the early church took the Gospel proclamation (Mark 16:2) and made the timeless truth the first day of the week. Sunday, the day Jesus arose from the dead, would be their new Sabbath. Early Christians would gather to observe the Lord's Supper on the day he arose from the grave. The understanding of what counted as observing the Lord's day thus evolved and continues to evolve. In the centuries since the church started observing Sunday as the Sabbath the human desire to regulate how to keep the Sabbath holy was revisited by almost every generation.

I grew up in a commonwealth that had "blue laws." These were legislated ordinances that dictated which businesses could be open on Sunday mornings and which ones had to be closed until at least noon. Over the years I encountered numerous churches that created similar "blue laws," or complicated lists of things that could be done and not done on Sunday. Some churches insisted that their members drive to church for morning and evening worship services (this kind of driving was not considered work) and then forbade their members from reading the newspaper or working on their cars on Sunday (this was unacceptable work). Other congregations demanded their pastors deliver several sermons and a Sunday school lesson on Sunday (this counted as acceptable work) while they forbade their members from watching television or doing housework, as each was deemed unnecessary work on their Sabbath. Like the religious leaders of the first century, honoring God was measured in the keeping of prescribed rules. To keep them would ensure God's blessings. To violate the rules would certainly incur the wrath of the church leaders if not God himself.

In contrast, there were folks who, like Jesus twenty centuries before, attempted to redefine what honoring God on the Sabbath meant. It is interesting to note that these committed people chose to make Jesus' words about not conforming to rules as their timeless truths. They felt justified in doing acts of caring and kindness for people even on Sunday. I observed Christians who performed acts of service on Sunday for neighbors or friends. I knew of people who chose to witness to the Bible's teachings by being involved in little league football and baseball leagues even when the games were played on Sunday afternoons. These faithful men and women were often confronted with hostility similar to the kind that Jesus received. Although no one I knew ended up being crucified, the keepers of the modern rules made life very difficult for those who dared to make timeless truths out of Jesus' text rather than their own.

Here we are, twenty-one centuries after Jesus, and there are new rules to be followed about keeping the new Sabbath holy. No Christian groups seem to utilize any of the sacrifices prescribed in Leviticus. All those prescriptions are seen as cultural norms that applied to the children of Israel but not to the modern world. There are people who perceive timeless truth is in the verses that prescribe not doing work. Others have made Jesus' words the timeless truths, where people can choose how to honor God on the Sabbath. Which Bible passages do you make into timeless truths about honoring God on the day of rest? Which verses will you treat as cultural norms? The timeless truth texts will define how we honor God on our Sabbath. Which texts do you use?

© David Hughes | Dreamstime.com

Case Study Four: **Scripture Remodeling Scripture on Death**

According to the Bible there are several explanations of what happens when we die. If we begin in the Hebrew Testament, death is simply the end. Abraham receives the promise that his name will live forever in the offspring that will follow him. His eternal life would be lived through future generations carrying his name. The ancient Hebrew culture did not differentiate between body and spirit. Both were one and were inseparable; when you died, your body and spirit died, too. The importance of having male offspring to carry on your name was a major reason so many provisions were made to make sure that every man had a male offspring.

As we move forward in time we see some developments in the biblical views about death. The ninth-century BCE prophet Elijah does not experience death according to the text in 2 Kings. However, his departure in a fiery chariot and whirlwind is a unique rendering both for the time and in terms of the image offered. Most Hebrews would have had no idea where he went other than to the firmament above the earth.

In the seventh century BCE we read some emerging references to a place of afterlife called *sheol*. For instance, Proverbs 9:18 says, "The fellow does not realize that here the Shades are gathered, that her guests are heading for the valleys of Sheol." (Jerusalem Bible) We also find the word *sheol* mentioned in Deuteronomy 32: "Yes, a fire has blazed from my anger, it will burn to the depths of Sheol." (Jerusalem Bible 22a). *Sheol* seems to be an emerging concept in the time Israel is in captivity. What is *sheol*? In Hebrew it was written to be the abode of the dead. Since the body and spirit were considered one, once the body had decayed there was not much left to be experienced. *Sheol* became known as a place deep within the earth (Pss. 88:5–6).

In the second century BCE, in the writing sometimes attributed to Queholeth, we clearly see the ancient thought has persisted. The teacher puts it quite bluntly: "For the living know that they will die, but the dead know nothing; they have no further reward, and even the memory of them is forgotten. Their love, their hate and their jealousy have long since vanished; never again will they have a part in anything that happens under the sun." (Eccles. 9:5–6). For the author, life is now and death is nothingness. If this text is made a timeless truth, then there is no need to consider eternity. It also suggests that how you live your life now is all that matters because this is all you get. In contrast to this oldest Hebrew view, we have an emerging awareness among the people of Israel that maybe there is more to life than the present.

Around the time of Daniel (175 BCE) we find the Hebrew Testament's first referral to eternal life: "Multitudes who sleep in the dust of the earth will awake; some to everlasting life, others to shame and everlasting contempt." (Dan. 12:2). Obviously, the children of Israel having spent hundreds of years in servitude resulted in the integration of some other thoughts about life and life after death. By the time we get to Jesus, there are two very distinct groups teaching two very different outlooks on death.

The Sadducees, a highly educated, aristocratic political and religious party, continued the ancient view that life is lived here and now and the body and spirit die together, period. In Mark 12 we read the fascinating story of Jesus' encounter with this group. They ask Jesus a hypothetical question about marriage in heaven and Mark wants us to know that the inquisitors don't even believe in a heaven, He writes, "Then the Sadducees, who say there is no resurrection, came to him with a question..." (Mark 12:18).

In contrast, the Pharisees, another religious political party, had adopted an outlook that includes life after death. As Greek philosophy and thought became more prevalent in the first century, its influence became more widely accepted. Their perception was that a person has a spirit that is separate from the body. This spirit takes on a life of its own when the body ceases to exist. In other words, when the physical body dies, the spirit, which continues to live, would go on to another place. This Greek view began to influence people throughout the Mediterranean world. The early church was no exception.

A verse that is often quoted concerning the body and spirit separating is found toward the end of Jesus' crucifixion experience recorded in Luke 23:43. The text reads, "Jesus answered him, 'I tell you the truth, today you will be with me in paradise.'" Jesus informs the penitent criminal that there would be a life after their grueling death. Many folks have made this a timeless truth and have come to believe that when a person's physical body dies, the spirit within it is liberated and sent to paradise to be with God. Obviously, after Jesus died his physical body was prepared for burial, although hastily, before being placed in the borrowed tomb. His spirit was gone, but his body was not. The two were reunited three days later. The post resurrection appearances found in John 20, Mark 16, Luke 24, and Matthew 28 each suggest that Jesus was in his recognizable body again, but that his spirit enabled him to transcend walls and doors in ways he had not done before. His ascension into heaven certainly parallels the prophet Elijah's departure, both physically and in spirit, to heaven. If these verses are considered timeless truths then we have a strong biblical case for believing that the body and spirit are separable, just as the Greeks suggested.

John's Gospel reveals even more ideas about what life after death would be like. Written toward the end of the first century CE, the author lays out many of the images the Christian church has made into timeless truths. In John 14 we find the portrait of heaven as having many dwelling places. (I always preferred the rendering "mansions") By the end of the first century the writer of Revelation put the cap on the images of what heaven would be like. In chapter 21 the Holy City with God present descends from the sky. The author promises that in the Holy City there will be no more pain, no more suffering, no tears, no death, and no mourning, for all these old things would have passed away. The new city will be brilliant as a jewel, with clear, crystal, high

walls and twelve gates. What an amazing picture. Again, many
Christians have made this text a timeless truth and that is exactly what
they anticipate heaven will be like. But the writer of Revelation also
draws a graphic picture of the eternal suffering awaiting those who are
judged and found wanting. Revelation 21 also describes a "fiery lake
of burning sulfur. This is the second death." If these passages are each
made into timeless truth walls in the house of biblical interpretation,
the images of where people go after death seem pretty clear. There are,
however, some conflicting Bible texts to reckon with.

To the scribes Jesus tells a parable that references eternal life. In Luke
16:19–31 we find the story of Dives, the rich man, and the poor man
Lazarus. The rich man ignores the poor beggar in the earthly life and
when they both die, the rich man finds himself in Hades and Lazarus
is in heaven. The rich man is able to communicate with Jesus but is
informed there is a gulf between their worlds that cannot be crossed.
Some folks have made the "reversals of fortunes" story into a timeless
truth. They have deduced that heaven and hell are separated and that
the two worlds cannot be bridged. Can people in hell really communicate
with those in heaven or is that portion of the story not to be taken
literally? If this text is perceived as a timeless truth, then no one in hell
can ever get out.

There are those who disagree with the above assertion. The question is
sometimes asked, what about those people who lived before the time
of Jesus, the people who never got a chance to hear about Christ?
Why didn't they get a chance to experience Christ's forgiveness and
eternal life? The early church response was found in 1 Peter 3:18–19,
which reads, "For Christ died for sins once for all, the righteous for
the unrighteous, to bring you to God. He was put to death in the
body but made alive by the Spirit, through whom also he went and
preached to the spirits in prison." The early church interpreted this
verse to mean that during the three days that Jesus' body was in the

tomb, his spirit was preaching to the captives in eternal prison. The Apostles' Creed picked up on this idea, directing believers to say, "I believe in Jesus Christ. . . . He suffered under Pontius Pilate, was crucified, died, and was buried. He descended into hell. On the third day he rose again . . ." According to these traditions the captives were given the opportunity to repent and receive God's forgiveness. For anyone who makes these verses and the resulting creed timeless truths, then it would be possible for the eternal captives to be freed from their damnation.

There is yet another image the Bible offers when it comes to what happens when people die. There are ample Bible references that compare death to sleep. That is the message Jesus gave the families he blessed with the miracle of bringing a loved one back to life. See, for example, Matt. 9:24, Mark 5:39, Luke 8:52, and John 11:11. If death is like sleep it is merely a temporary state that the body goes through before it wakes up. Paul wrote the Thessalonican church these words: "Brothers, we do not want you to be ignorant about those who fall asleep, or to grieve like the rest of men who have no hope. We believe that Jesus died and rose again and so we believe that God will bring with Jesus those who have fallen asleep in him" (1 Thess. 4:13–14). Then Paul goes on to say that those who are dead in Christ will be awakened "with the voice of the archangel and with the trumpet call of God, and the dead in Christ will rise first" (1 Thess. 4:16b). This would imply that the dead in Christ may still have their spirits with them, albeit "asleep," and then when Christ comes, their bodies and spirits would awaken and join the heavenly throngs and be with the Lord forever. As you can see, this is certainly a different portrait than a person's spirit being welcomed into heaven immediately. Some might ask, which is it? Does the spirit stay with the body (Jewish thought) and stay asleep until Jesus returns? Or does the spirit immediately leave the body and join God in heaven? That is where you get to decide. Which verses will you choose to designate a wall of timeless truth in your house of biblical interpretation? Which text will you see as a non-binding cultural norm or personal opinion? Obviously, both images are presented in the Bible. Can they both be true at the same time? You will have to decide. As you construct your house of biblical interpretation, which verses will be timeless truth walls and which will merely be the paint or decorations?

If we consider what happens to physical bodies after we die we soon discover there are multiple images presented in the Bible as well. When Jesus raised Lazarus and Jairus' daughter they each came back with the same body and the same spirit. There is no mention that their resuscitated bodies could do anything new or different. In each of their cases, they lived to eventually die again. However, if we consider Jesus' personal experience, we see that he came back to a similar body (his friends eventually recognized him) but it could do things his previous body could not. In John 20 we read that Jesus was able to enter a locked room apparently without using the door. Yet, he invited his disciple Thomas to touch his pierced hands and side. If this verse were to be considered a timeless truth, it would suggest our earthly scars do not go away in our heavenly body. This text, if taken literally, would suggest Jesus could metaphysically go through walls yet his wounds were not gone. What really happens to the body, we may ask.

The apostle Paul describes a new heavenly body in 1 Corinthians 15, implying that the heavenly body will be different. He says, "the splendor of the heavenly bodies is one kind, and the splendor of the earthly bodies is another." If we consider these texts timeless truths, then we will see new bodies when we get to heaven. How will we recognize each other? Will we even notice each other if we are in God's holy presence? It should be apparent that no one description is offered as a timeless truth. Since there is biblical witness to a variety of beliefs, God has given us the freedom to be our own architects as we design our houses of biblical interpretation. We readers of the Bible are invited to read, discern, and eventually choose what we believe happens to our spirits and our earthly bodies after we die. The texts we make timeless truths will determine the way we live.

Would you be interested in doing more reading and research? Check out Revelation 20:11–15. What interpretation does the white throne judgment suggest? If you read 1 Corinthians 15, what interpretation does the apostle Paul offer? Now read 2 Corinthians 12:2. What does the apostle Paul suggest about heaven? Do you agree with him or not?

Case Study Five: **An Apostle Remodels Scripture**

In Genesis 9 God makes a covenant with Noah and promises that he and his family, and they alone, will be saved. When God destroys all the other people for their wickedness, God remembers Noah. Generations later we find God choosing Abram and promising to make him into a great nation. Genesis 12 reveals the terms of the covenant that is to be Abram's exclusively. In fact, all nations will get their own blessing through Abram. Surely, Abram is the father of all the children of God.

In Genesis 17 God reinterprets the covenant with Abram by giving him a new name, Abraham, and giving him an exclusive sign— circumcision—whereby "Every male among you shall be circumcised. You are to undergo circumcision, and it will be the sign of the covenant between me and you. For generations to come every male among you who is eight days old must be circumcised." This sign would be the exclusive mark of God's chosen people forever forward. For those who consider these texts timeless truths, circumcision is to be the sign that must be part of a child of God's life. By the time of Jesus, the children of Israel were still distinguished by their covenant of circumcision. Jesus himself was circumcised on the eighth day (Luke 2) and when the early church was born on the streets of Jerusalem as described in Acts 2, Paul and other disciples encountered a great deal of discussion about the role circumcision should play, particularly for non-Jewish, Gentile followers of Jesus. Indeed, in Acts 15, we read that the Jerusalem church is forced to debate what role circumcision will play for Gentile believers. The Pharisee followers of Jesus argue that to be a true child of God the Gentile converts must first be circumcised. After all, the timeless, truth texts of Genesis 17 cannot be ignored; even Jesus observed them.

In contrast, Paul and Peter argue that the Genesis 17 text is not meant to be a timeless truth for Gentiles but rather merely describes a non-binding cultural norm. The two apostles speak authoritatively, claiming that they witnessed the Spirit of God already at work among the Gentiles in Antioch and that circumcision was not necessary for the Spirit to work among them. Can you imagine the emotion in these men as each passionately presented his views? Although no record is given of what was actually said, I can imagine the two sides heatedly scolding one another. "How dare you possibly think you can change a thousand years of history," the Pharisees might have said. "Yes, we can reinterpret the present," Peter and Paul might have countered, "because the Spirit is showing us a new reality. God is doing a new thing." I imagine the tension was at a fever pitch when James finally reaches his verdict. He declares, "It is my judgment, therefore, that we should not make it difficult for the Gentiles who are turning to God" (Acts 15:19). James then tells the assembly that the Gentiles do not have to be circumcised. Notice that no vote was taken. In fact, what happened in that moment was profound. Over one thousand years of tradition was instantly reinterpreted. The holy scriptures in Genesis 17 were moved from timeless truth status to cultural norm status for the Gentiles and the early church. James made the decision himself with wisdom from the Holy Spirit. His action demonstrates that God can change the rules, even though the verses in the text that support a different interpretation do not go away. The Spirit was able to lead James to reinterpret the scriptures in a whole new way. Genesis 17 to this day remains a timeless truth for Jews. However, the same text is merely a cultural norm that Gentile followers of Jesus can choose to ignore.

I believe the Acts 15 account is a landmark, ground breaking case. I think it demonstrates that in God's world, which is our world, the Spirit of God can move unrestricted by the interpretations of the holy scriptures and traditions of the past. The Spirit chose to work in Antioch before the disciples got there. The Spirit chose to change Paul's and Peter's perceptions about where the Spirit could work long before the assembly met in Jerusalem. When the Spirit is at work, Bible texts that were considered timeless truths even for generations can be remodeled and given new status. Like Genesis 17, a Bible passage can move to another category and the house of biblical interpretation will not collapse. God's grace still saves those whom God chooses. In fact, the new room arrangement will make God's house less difficult to live in for the recipients of God's grace. In the case of the church in Antioch, the converts who chose to follow Jesus would not have to experience painful circumcision in order to be a child of God. I imagine they praised God for that decision!

Are there texts you know that apply to one group of followers of Jesus and not to another? In your faith experience are there Bible verses that you have seen apply to your group but not to a friend's group? List some of those texts.

Case Study Six: God: Inclusive or Exclusive?

How inclusive is God? Obviously, it depends on which passages of the Bible you turn to for timeless truth "proof." I begin with Genesis 1:27–31, where God has created male and female at the same time and blessed each of them and given them the mandate, "Be fruitful and increase in number, fill the earth and subdue it" (Gen. 1:28). Male and female are each created in the image of God and each given an equal charge to procreate and dominate the creation. From here the Hebrew text offers an interesting assortment of texts that, when each is made into a timeless truth, can radically influence history.

In Genesis 9 the flood is over and the world is being repopulated. The sons of Noah are listed as Shem, Ham, and Japheth. Historically this simple text provides some interesting insights. Shem is afforded a special blessing in verse 26: "Blessed be the Lord, the God of Shem! May Canaan be the slave of Shem."

Shem was perceived to be the ancestor of all Semitic people. Ham, who was cursed in verse 25 for having seen his father's nakedness (Gen. 9:22), was perceived to be the father of the people of Canaan, Cush, Egypt, and the African continent. Ham's descendants were cursed to be the slaves of Shem; believe it or not, this was the biblical basis for the enslavement of Africans during the eighteenth and nineteenth centuries. When Genesis 9:26 was established as a timeless truth, and Ham's descendants were attributed Africans, the interpreters could justify the slave trade using this Bible verse.

Japheth, the third son, was believed to be the father of the people around the Black Sea, Asia Minor, and eventually all of Europe. This would trace all the people of the ancient world to a beginning in the Bible. In Genesis 11 we find the origin of the diverse languages of the world, as the tower of Babel story sought to explain their beginning.

By Genesis 16 we find the stories of Abraham and Hagar creating Ishmael and all the people we know in the modern world as Arabic. In Genesis 21 Abraham and Sarah begat Isaac and the lineage of the Hebrew people is begun. Can there be any doubt that the writers of the Hebrew Testament are tracing all people back to their God? But God's inclusiveness is not just found in the generic creation of all people and language groups.

In the book of Joshua, Rahab, a foreigner and prostitute from Jericho, is given special status among the Hebrews because of the assistance she gave the Jewish spies. Ruth, a Moabite, is given permission to marry a Jewish landowner named Boaz. They will be forerunners of the great king David. In the prophet Isaiah's eighth-century BCE world anyone who sought God would find him (Isa. 56). In the book of the minor prophet Jonah, God wants to include the inhabitants of the foreign city of Nineveh among his people and sends Jonah to bring them into God's fold. God then includes them, because they responded affirmatively to Jonah's message. The minor prophet Joel tells his ninth-century BCE audience that in the day of the Lord, "I will pour out my spirit on all people, your sons and daughters will prophesy, your old men will dream dreams, your young men will see visions, even on my servants, both men and women I will pour out my Spirit in those days" (Joel 2:28–29). And in verse 32 of chapter 2 Joel tells us, "And everyone who calls on the name of the Lord will be saved." What an amazing promise. Anyone, from any nationality or language group, of either gender, of any economic status—anyone—who calls on the Lord will be saved. If these verses are perceived as timeless truths, then the Spirit of God can and will save any and all who call upon the Lord's name. Please keep in mind, these verses were written seven to eight hundred years before Christ. God was including all kinds of people long before the Greek Testament came along.

The Greek Testament generates even more movement showing God's inclusiveness. Matthew 25 records the apocalyptic picture of God drawing the people from all the nations of the earth before the judgment seat. Then God separates the believers from the nonbelievers of all nations. This would suggest there are believers in all nations. In Matthew 28 the Christian church is given what has become known as the Great Commission: "Therefore, go and make disciples of all nations . . ." (Matt. 28:19). There are no boundaries given nor any limitations drawn. The people of the world need to hear about God's love for them. John 3:16 tells us, "For God so loved the world that he gave his one and only Son." Again, no restrictions are made. The people of the world need to hear the good news that God loves them, that Jesus forgives them, and that the Spirit of God wants to empower them. How will the world hear about this?

In Acts 2 the Holy Spirit descends on the followers of Jesus in Jerusalem. One of the results of the Spirit's arrival is that the Galileans are given the ability to speak languages from around the world so that visitors in Jerusalem (from around the world) could hear the gospel of Jesus in their own language. In Acts 8 Philip receives a vision and is led to talk to an Ethiopian eunuch who is leaving Jerusalem. After being baptized, the Ethiopian takes the gospel of Jesus back to Africa. In Acts 10 Peter is prepared to minister to the Roman Cornelius' household. The inferred result is that the Roman centurion would take the gospel of Jesus back to his people. The remainder of the book of Acts recounts Paul's multiple missionary journeys to Asia Minor, Greece, Rome, and the text even hints that he traveled to Spain. The world was the target, and God found creative and unique ways and diverse people to get the message out. Why? Because God desires to be inclusive of all people everywhere. Paul summarizes the inclusivity of God in Romans 10:13 when he says, "Everyone who calls on the name of the Lord will be saved." If these texts are considered timeless truths, then there are no groups of people that God does not want to include. All will be welcomed as they call upon the name of the Lord.

I know people who disagree with this theology of inclusivity. They may be literalists or they may be old school thinkers. Nonetheless, they take a very different stance when it comes to who can and will be included in the kingdom of God than I suggest here. For these folks, who I call exclusivists, believe there are lots of people who will not be included in the kingdom of God for a variety of reasons that the Bible delineates. Exclusivists believe that certain biblical passages, such as Romans 1:18, which says, "The wrath of God is being revealed from heaven against all the godlessness and wickedness of men who suppress the truth by their wickedness," are timelessly true. Those who are wicked will not be included in the kingdom of God, "just as there will be false teachers among you. They will secretly introduce destructive heresies, even denying the sovereign Lord who bought them—bringing swift destruction on themselves. Many will follow their shameful ways and will bring the way of truth into disrepute" (2 Peter 2:1–2). And so false teachers who corrupt the teaching of Christ will not be included in the kingdom of God either. Nor will the followers who blindly follow their destructive heresies and false teachings. Exclusive folks agree with the writer of Jude, who warned his first-century audience, "For certain men whose condemnation was written about long ago have secretly slipped in among you. They are godless men, who change the grace of our God into a license for immorality and deny Jesus Christ our only Sovereign and Lord" (Jude 1:4). Exclusivists are certain those who use the grace of God as a license for immorality must be considered outside the timeless truth walls of God's inclusiveness. Anyone who would deny Christ cannot receive the inclusivity God has offered to people.

Another group to be excluded would be those who lead others astray, especially children. The words from Matthew 18 issue this stern warning: "But if anyone causes one of these little ones who believe in me to sin, it would be better for him to have a large millstone hung around his neck and to be drowned in the depths of the sea." Note there is no inclusive grace suggested in these texts. If these verses are timeless truths texts, then there is only punishment ahead for those who fail to heed the warnings. Such people will certainly be excluded from God's kingdom on earth and in the life to come.

There are other texts that may suggest God's grace is not going to include everyone. I know exclusivists who argue that unless people "flee from sexual immorality" (1 Cor. 6:18) the inclusive grace of God cannot touch the offender. For people taking this interpretive line, the Greek Testament texts found in Matthew 7 are particularly important. Here, the author writes, "Enter through the narrow gate. For wide is the gate and broad is the road that leads to destruction, and many enter through it. But small is the gate and narrow the road that leads to life, and only a few find it." According to this way of thinking, the path to being included in God's inclusiveness is highly selective and few will qualify. When these verses are made timeless truths, the inclusive texts gain the status of cultural norm or personal opinion. For the exclusive person the threat of false teachers will manifest itself in people who look like innocent sheep but who, underneath the seductive exterior, embrace a dangerous theology or ideology. To justify their stance, exclusive thinkers point to verses like this one: "Not everyone who says to me, Lord, Lord, will enter the kingdom of heaven, but only he who does the will of my Father who is in heaven" (Matt. 7:21). Simply claiming that God is Lord is not good enough to earn God's grace, according to an exclusivist interpretation of this text. Just doing mighty acts in God's name is not enough either. Matthew provides this test: "By their fruit you will recognize them. . . . A good tree cannot bear bad fruit, and a bad tree cannot bear good fruit. Every tree that does not bear good fruit is cut down and thrown into the fire" (Matt. 7:16-19). Judgment is imminent for the producers of bad fruit. To reinforce the importance of the fruit, exclusive thinkers often recite the verses Matthew uses to describe the final judgment. People standing before Jesus are quoted as saying, "'Did we not prophesy in your name, and in your name drive out demons and perform many miracles?' Then I will tell them plainly, 'I never knew you; away from me, you evildoers!'" (Matt. 7:22–23). Jesus' warning is a sobering statement, exclusive proponents tell us. There will be people who have done amazing miracles and dazzled crowds with their spiritual feats, yet a person doing the impressive act may not have a personal relationship with Jesus. Jesus will then judge them not according to the impressive things they have done, but on their failure to develop a relationship with him. These charlatans in the faith will be told they are not included.

When the texts about judgment are the primary verses regarded as timeless truths, the possibility of inclusivity is, for the most part, lost. There is a strong old school flavor to these texts. If you believe and behave . . . then you will find the path. If you disobey or disbelieve the truth . . . then you will be judged and found wanting. Destruction lies ahead. Exclusive thinkers have these and other selected texts that they hold as timeless truths. In their minds these texts take priority over the inclusive texts mentioned earlier.

Both sets of texts are found in the library we call the Bible. Clearly there are verses speaking of God's inclusive desire in "not wanting anyone to perish, but everyone to come to repentance" (2 Pet. 3:9). There are also those verses that express that "nothing impure will ever enter it [heaven] nor will anyone who does what is shameful or deceitful, but only those whose names are written in the Lamb's book of life" (Rev. 21:27). Which set of texts fit with the church experience you had growing up? Which approach fits the church you are in now?

Which one captures what you think personally? Is the inclusive nature of God or the judgmental exclusive nature more foundational in your house of biblical interpretation? Whichever texts you choose as your timeless truths will dictate how you both live and view others.

Case Study Seven: **Traditional Grace vs. Realist Radical Grace**

In the world of biblical interpretation one current issue has generated more energy than almost any other in recent memory. The issue: the role homosexual men and women are allowed to play in the life of Christian churches. There are at least two very opposite and passionately held stances on this issue. One I label traditional grace. The other I call realist radical grace. I will address each of the stances using the tools of this book. As you move ahead in this case study I would like you to keep in mind a couple important facts.

First, please note that I will no longer be using the word "homosexual" in this case study. The word never appears in the original manuscripts of the Bible. In fact, the first time the word ever appears in a Bible is in the 1952 version of the Revised Standard Version (RSV). Whenever possible I will attempt to use the words that are closest to the original language translation. Second, I want to allow the tools of this book to set the stage for a dialogue. Therefore, I encourage you as the reader to go all the way through the case study in order to hear the different uses of the biblical texts. Probably each reader will find an interpretation that he or she agrees with. I hope you do not just stop at the point where you find this agreement. Instead, I encourage you to read through to the end, seeking to understand the viewpoints and biblical interpretations that are different from your own. It is my desire to have the diverse viewpoints understood better. I think the tools this book presents give us a forum to talk about our personal stands on this issue.

Let's start with the traditional grace perspective. It has been my observation that this viewpoint has had an iron grip on how the Bible verses are interpreted. Remember, traditional thinking is based on an "if/then" approach to interpreting faith. Leviticus 20:13 reads, "If a man lies with a man as one lies with a woman, both of them have done what is detestable. They must be put to death; their blood will be on their own heads." The text seems pretty black and white. To the traditional grace proponents there is no wiggle room in this Bible text. Using the traditional formula, we get this: If a man lies with a man, then it is detestable to God. If a man has sex with a man, then they are both to be put to death. Although the text does not mention women lying with women, most readers tend to imply lesbian acts are equally detestable to God and deserve the same death sentence. If this verse is considered literally timeless truths, same-sex offenders should be put to death. There are gay bashers who have taken this verse literally and chosen to kill men or women just because they were gay. Although same-sex acts are believed to be detestable to God, even the most conservative, traditional Christians have not condoned the brutal killings, but the condemnation of the same-sex person has often been upheld.

The Greek Testament presents another text that traditional grace thinkers view as an equally clear condemnation of same-sex behavior. The apostle Paul describes same-sex acts and the people who engage in them in Romans 1:26–27 this way: "God gave them over to shameful lusts. Even their women exchanged natural relations for unnatural ones. In the same way the men also abandoned natural relations with women and were inflamed with lust for one another. Men committed indecent acts with other men, and received in themselves the due penalty for their perversion." For traditional grace thinkers this is more reinforcement. It is unnatural for men or women to do sexual acts with people of their own gender. If these acts between people of the same sex come out of a lustful desire . . . then they will receive a penalty for their perversion. For some traditional grace proponents,

HIV and AIDS are perceived to be the penalty God inflicted on gay men for their detestable actions. If this text in Romans is perceived as a timeless truth wall in the house of biblical interpretation, there is no way a same-sex person can be viewed as anything but unnatural and perverted. For churches that have taken these verses as the final word or the timeless biblical truth about same-sex behavior, their walls keep gay and lesbian people out, and their doors are closed to people of gay and lesbian behavior. Gay and lesbian people are not welcome to worship, to join, to commune, or serve these churches.

There is a less harsh traditional grace attitude that also maintains that the Leviticus and Romans texts are definitive about same-sex behavior as unnatural and perverted. However, they have accepted the fact that gay and lesbian individuals can have a relationship with God. They recognize Romans 10:9, which says, "That if you confess with your mouth, 'Jesus is Lord', and believe in your heart that God raised him from the dead, you will be saved." This verse does not exclude anyone based on his or her sexual behavior. So these church people believe that gay and lesbian people who confess Jesus as Lord and believe in their hearts that he was raised from the dead will be saved. However, they also proclaim that a gay or lesbian person cannot go on sinning. For these traditional grace advocates 1 Corinthians 6:18 is an important corollary timeless truth. It says, "Flee from sexual immorality. All other sins a man commits are outside his body, but he who sins sexually sins against his own body." If gay or lesbian people flee from same-sex actions, then they will not be sinning against their bodies. These churches often welcome gay and lesbian people, but the expectation is that these men and women must live celibate sexual lives. If you do not participate in same-sex activity and you confess Jesus as Lord and believe in his resurrection, then you are saved and you can attend their church.

A third traditional grace approach holds the Leviticus and Romans texts as timeless truths. They have put a different verse in the mix of timeless truths, however. That is 2 Corinthians 12:7–8. Here, Paul writes, "There was given me a thorn in my flesh, a messenger of Satan, to torment me. Three times I pleaded with the Lord to take it away from me. But he said to me 'My grace is sufficient for you, for my power is made perfect in weakness.'" This traditional grace perspective suggests that each person may have a thorn in his or her flesh, a battle to fight that is challenging. This way of thinking suggests that the thorn in the flesh for gay and lesbian people is their orientation to people of the same gender. These same-sex folks may have prayed for deliverance from the orientation, but if God did not take it away, then it is their thorn with which to wrestle. God's grace will be sufficient for them in spite of their same-sex affinity. This is the challenge they must face every day. If their thorns do not go away, then they must live with them. This line of thinking is supported by another important verse that is regarded as timeless truths: "The body is not meant for sexual immorality, but for the Lord, and the Lord for the body" (1 Cor. 6:13b). Indulging in same-sex behavior would be immoral. If gay men or lesbian women do not practice same-sex behavior, then they can be members of the church. They might be limited in what ministries they can do, but they will be welcome nonetheless.

For some readers the above description of the traditional grace stance seems biblically correct. The verses referred to reveal the only true understanding of how the Bible views same-sex relationships. For others, this interpretation has been the source of pain and anguish be-yond measure. This may be especially true for gay and lesbian people who have experienced the closed church door, the conditional accep-tance, or the limited roles that traditional grace members of the church have laid out for them. Individuals, pastors, and congregations that have tried to be more welcoming to gay and lesbian people have often received harsh words and condemning statements as a result of their position. The traditional grace advocates have not tended to place a welcome mat out for anyone who disagrees with their walls of interpretation. Is there another approach within the Bible itself that might lead us to a different set of conclusions? I invite you to read on and see what else the Bible says. You may be surprised.

The realist radical grace stance also has a biblical basis. It is rooted in the understanding that there are situations in the Bible that demonstrate how accepted traditions and ancient interpretations of scripture were reinterpreted. The fact that the reinterpretations took place in the first century gives the modern reader the opportunity to see how the remodeling of established walls of timeless truth was done. The changes we will look at were all God's idea. The remodeling took place with the Spirit of God's direction often in spite of human reluctance to accept the changes. We begin the look at realist radical grace position in Paul's letter to the Corinthians.

In 1 Corinthians 2 Paul tells the young church that God's Spirit does not always conform to accepted wisdom. He says, "This is what we speak, not in words taught us by human wisdom but in words taught by the Spirit, expressing spiritual truths in spiritual words. The man without the Spirit does not accept the things that come from the Spirit of God, for they are foolishness to him and he cannot understand them" (1 Cor. 2:13–14). In this passage, Paul lets his readers know that the Spirit of God at times leads the people of God in new directions, directions that people who are not tuned into the Spirit do not accept. In fact, to people who are caught up in their traditions or their own interpretations of the Bible, the direction in which the Spirit of God is leading people will look downright foolish. The believers who are insensitive to the Spirit's direction will prefer following the well-worn path of traditional interpretation rather than embark on the uncharted course to which the Spirit is pointing.

Let's take a look at a perfect example in the Greek Testament. In Acts 10, the author, Luke, tells two stories about the movement of the Spirit of God. First, the Spirit of God appears in the home of a man named Cornelius considered by first-century Jewish Christians to be an unclean Gentile. Early first-century Jewish Christians would have been aghast at the thought of such a visit. The accepted human understanding at the time was that God would never appear to an unclean Gentile. That just would not happen. However, the Spirit of God, defying accepted thought, visits Cornelius and directs the Roman centurion to send for Peter, who was in the city of Joppa. Simultaneously, the Spirit of God appears to an exhausted, hungry Peter who has fallen asleep on the roof of the home where he is staying. The apostle falls into a deep sleep and has a dream. The dream is very disturbing for Peter. A sheet comes down from heaven filled with animals that are unclean—food that was specifically forbidden from the Jewish diet. Then a voice tells Peter, "'Get up, Peter, kill and eat'" (Acts 10:13). Peter, drawing on his earthly wisdom, speaks back, "Surely not, Lord! . . . I have never eaten anything impure or unclean" (Acts 10:14). Peter was an observant Jew. He had read the scriptures and he knew Leviticus 20:25, which says, "You must therefore make a distinction between clean and unclean animals and between unclean and clean birds. Do not defile yourselves by any animal or bird or anything that moves along the ground--those which I have set apart as unclean for you." Peter could see no wiggle room in this Hebrew Testament injunction. It commanded people not eat anything on the unclean list or they would be defiled. Peter boldly, if not even proudly, tells God that he would never break that ancient command, that he would never defile himself by breaking the Levitical code. What happened next was blasphemy to many first-century Jewish Christian readers. The Spirit of God says to Peter, "Do not call anything impure that God has made clean" (Acts 10:15). Had God changed the rulebook from the Hebrew Testament? No; it still read that these foods were unclean. In an effort to defend his own understanding Peter quotes the Bible back to God! "'Surely not, Lord!'" (Acts 10:14a). The Spirit, however, goes on and insists that these animals are now acceptable to eat. Apparently Peter could not get the message past his biases very quickly, as the Spirit goes through the whole exercise three times. (There must be something about the number three with Peter: three denials, three "feed my sheep," and now three visions.) The dream was not going to take place literally. Peter would not be asked to actually kill and eat the animals. However, the message from the Spirit of God to Peter was that as a disciple of Jesus, Peter would need to be prepared to treat people who would be considered unclean according to the traditional, Hebrew human understanding as clean because of God's Spirit. The people in question would not have conformed to any of the holiness codes, the festivals, or the lifestyle choices that were considered important by the early church leaders. The vision was preparing Peter for the visitors who were about to arrive.

Peter discovered firsthand how the Spirit of God could lead in a direction that conventional wisdom would consider foolish. Yet, it was the Spirit leading. It was the Spirit telling Peter there was a new interpretation happening beginning at that moment. Peter was defiant at first and then reluctant to accept the new directive from God.

The next day Cornelius' servants arrive at Peter's house and Peter chooses to follow the Spirit's lead. He goes with the Gentile men to minister to Cornelius' Gentile household. Peter had been told by the Spirit that he could no longer call anything (anyone) impure or unclean that God had made clean. This is an incredible picture of realist radical grace at work. An unclean Gentile family is pronounced clean by the Spirit. And Peter reluctantly accepts the Spirit's decision. The application of this principle to our modern day example would be this: When the Spirit of God has touched the life of a person with same-sex feelings, this person is no longer impure or unclean in God's eyes. Yes, the Levitical passages are still in the Bible, but the Spirit of God is leading the people of God to a new understanding. According to this realist radical grace interpretation, the church can no longer call impure or unclean what God has made clean. For proponents of realist radical grace, this text in Acts 10 is a timeless truth. That means the Spirit of God has led them to include gay and lesbian people as full members of the church.

But Paul has more to say. In Galatians 3 the apostle tells his first-century followers, "for all of you who were baptized into Christ have clothed yourselves with Christ. There is neither Jew nor Greek, slave nor free, male nor female, for you are all one in Christ Jesus" (Gal. 3:27–28). In Christ, the human distinctions that are so important and often divisive among people are all taken away. According to Paul there are no longer nationalities (there are neither Jews nor Greeks). There are no longer differences based on economic status (as slave or free). There are no longer gender distinctions (male or female). For realists this suggests that once a person has been baptized into Christ he or she becomes a new creation (2 Cor. 5:17). If God does not distinguish between nations or languages; if God does not reward the good with wealth and the bad with slavery; if God does not notice gender, then why would God care about a person's sexual orientation? For realist radical grace thinkers once the Spirit of God has touched a person's life that person will be cleansed by the Spirit. The Spirit has made gay and lesbian people just as clean as straight people who were unclean because they were thieves, idolaters, drunkards, slanderers, swindlers, liars, adulterers, or who had committed any of the countless other faults mentioned throughout the Bible. If the Spirit has made them clean then the same Spirit empowers gay and lesbian people. In Ephesians 4 Paul tells us, "There is one body and one Spirit—just as you were called to one hope when you were called—one Lord, one faith, one baptism, one God and Father of All, who is over all and through all and in all." That one Spirit who cleanses all also empowers all: "But to each one of us grace has been given as Christ apportioned it." Realists would suggest this means that gays and lesbians will be empowered by the Spirit with spiritual gifts that can build up the body of Christ and do the work of ministry in the world. Realist radical grace practices the empowerment of all its cleansed members. God does not differentiate between gay, lesbian, and straight cleansed people. They are all clean. They are all gifted. They are all called to use their gifts to build the kingdom of God. Realist radical grace empowers gifted men and women to lead worship, preach, teach, serve the sacraments, and counsel fellow members of the body of Christ. It will not matter from what fault they were cleansed. What matters is that the cleansed people use their gifts to further God's glory. When these verses are joined into making a wall of timeless truth, the room created will include gay, lesbian, and straight people equally. These churches will welcome all people, believing that the Spirit of God will lead them to be cleansed. These churches will use people based on their gifts and no restrictions will be made based on their status as gay, lesbian, straight, male, female, married, divorced, or any other. They are all new creatures in Christ.

For realist radical grace proponents, the Acts 10 text modeled what the Spirit of God did in the first century and can do in this century. In essence, the Holy Spirit can bring new interpretations to old verses. Peter had to overcome one thousand years of Jewish understanding to be obedient to the Spirit. And when he obeyed the Spirit he willfully broke the law he had been taught. So, too, realists believe they are called by the Spirit to a new interpretation of a two-thousand-year-old understanding. When churches practice this inclusive radical grace, Realists break from the accepted understanding that churches have upheld for millennium. However, Peter was told to obey the Spirit of God rather than the letter of the written law. In similar fashion, Realists may choose to follow the Spirit's lead rather than conform to the letter of the written law.

Luke makes a point of letting his readers know that Peter's decision to visit Cornelius was not well received by his local church. In Acts 11 we find out that he is severely criticized by the established Jerusalem church for taking the liberty of breaking the ancient traditional law and eating with the unclean. In the modern world Realist congregations know that kind of disapproval as well. To follow the Spirit in the new direction of radical grace often carries with it the disapproval of those upholding established views. Traditional proponents will verbally and sometimes even physically demonstrate their disapproval. Realists understand this is part of the cross they must bear. To follow the Spirit rather than tradition is risky. To include gays and lesbians as equally cleansed and gifted as all other people is blasphemy to some. To allow these Spirit-led Bible texts to take precedence over the traditional judgmental texts is even heresy to others. That is where the realist radical grace proponents come to claim Paul's words again: "The man without the Spirit does not accept the things that come from the Spirit of God, for they are foolishness to him, and he cannot understand them, because they are spiritually discerned" (1 Cor. 2:14).

These are the two views. The traditional grace view requires gay and lesbian people to quit practicing their sexuality, and by so doing receive no or only marginal ministry opportunities in the church. The realist radical grace view that says the Spirit has empowered and cleansed gay and lesbian people the same as it has all other cleansed people. Therefore, they can serve in full capacities as their gifts lead them in the Christian church. Which view is closest to your denomination's view? Which view is closest to that of your local church? What is your own view? If you had to respond to a traditional grace advocate what would you say? If you encountered a realist radical grace proponent what would you say? Do you think God can still change the interpretation of scripture the way he did in Acts 10? Now read Acts 15. What long-held tradition does God lead James to reinterpret?

© Richard Gunion | Dreamstime.com

Using the Tools *Together*

*W*hen we were planning to build our house in Stillwater, we
looked for a neighborhood that would have homes similar
to the one we were going to build. We found an empty lot that we
liked in a new development, and presented our plans to the city's

zoning authority and then to the development's covenant committee. Each group had to approve that our structure would be within the codes of that particular subdivision. Having passed those requirements we were free to build our house. In fact, ours was the first home built on the cul-de-sac. As part of a larger community we had the assurance that when other people wanted to build their homes on the vacant lots surrounding ours, they would be putting in similarly sized structures, and they would also need to comply with the development's building codes and covenants.

Although neighborhoods may look similar on the outside, very few of the houses are exactly the same. Neighborhoods can have buildings of the same exact shape, but each building may be painted a different external color. Similarly shaped structures may have interiors that are nothing alike. The interior walls may be placed differently, the decorating schemes may be different, and the furniture and knick-knacks not at all alike. In other words, very few places are exactly the same inside and out. Yet people live side by side without too much conflict. They don't expect every aspect of their homes to be duplicated. In fact, most people look for ways to make their homes distinctive, whether through design, color, landscaping, or some other distinguishing feature.

In many ways people do similar things after building their personal houses of biblical interpretation. Of course, people tend to seek to come together in communities of people who share similar values and who hold similar timeless truths. These gatherings can be called small groups, congregations, or even denominations. People who think similarly tend to be more comfortable with others who are of like minds. However, it would be unrealistic to think that every person in every church agrees about every interpretation of every text. There's just no way that would happen. It would even be hard to find one family in which all members agree about their interpretations of every text. In other words, the "homes" in our theological neighborhoods are probably as diverse on the inside as our neighborhood homes are. And just like our neighborhood homes, they may even differ on the outside. I would like to take a few moments to talk about how we as followers of Jesus can live in similar neighborhoods without totally agreeing on the interpretation of every biblical text.

The story of my college days that I first referenced in the introduction was an example of people with different interpretations living in the same scriptural neighborhood. As the war in Southeast Asia escalated in the 1960s, an influx of young men who came to serve arrived on our state college campus. Most of these fellows were from religious backgrounds that believed that people should not return evil for evil. The draft labeled them conscientious objectors (COs). These young men who were drafted by the government, instead of going to war, accepted a two-year assignment working within the university system of our commonwealth. They received the same pay as enlisted military personnel, and they worked in the cafeteria, the maintenance shed, the grounds department, or in janitorial jobs. Although the COs refused to take up military arms they offered their physical arms to do the less desirable tasks around campus. They were loyal to America in their willingness to serve their country. Yet they were loyal to their interpretation of scripture, too, and refused to do to another human being what they perceived as evil.

These COs joined us in our Christian Bible studies on campus, and there were many evenings when a ROTC (Reserve Officer Training Candidate) from the military armory nearby debated the Romans texts with the COs. The differences between the two interpretations were not erased during the conversations. Each person shared with deep convictions the stance he held so dear. Still, members of the group maintained a love and respect for one another. Neither side condemned the other as unchristian nor did they belittle the other's stance. They just agreed that the Spirit of God had led them to different conclusions. Each person lived according to the guidance of the text that he considered a timeless truth. How is that possible?

Speaking about the Spirit of God, Paul says, "But to each one of us grace has been given as Christ apportioned it" (Eph. 4:7). In other words, people are not given faith in exactly the same way. Paul goes on in the chapter to say that the same Spirit gives different gifts to different people. It only stands to reason that if the one Spirit can lead one person to be a pastor and another person to be a teacher, the same Spirit can lead one person to believe that he should serve his country in the military and another person that he should serve in a pacifist capacity. Furthermore, this passage implies that the same Spirit does not apportion faith equally to everyone, nor does the Spirit need to lead everyone to the same conclusions on every issue. When the Spirit is at work it is very possible that people can draw more than one conclusion. Let's look at a couple of biblical examples.

In Acts 15:36–41 we see an interesting example of conflict among the early church leaders. The setting is the preparation for a missionary journey that Barnabas and Paul were planning to take together. As they readied themselves for their departure each disciple suggested an associate to go along on the trip. Barnabas nominated John Mark. Paul disagreed. Apparently, John Mark had abandoned the team in Pamphylia causing Paul's lack of trust in the young man. In this story we see two fathers of the early church, Paul and Barnabas, disagreeing over John Mark's readiness for the missionary journey. The text reads, "They had such a sharp disagreement that they parted company. Barnabas took Mark and sailed for Cyprus, but Paul chose Silas and left." The one true Spirit of God led Barnabas to believe John Mark was ready for a missionary journey to Cyprus, while the same Spirit led Paul to the conclusion that John Mark was not ready to be part of his traveling staff. The same Spirit of God led two apostles to draw opposite conclusions. I believe this is an example of how the Spirit of God can work. Now, we could infer that Paul and Barnabas were just offering conflicting personal opinions. But I am sure each prayed about who they should take on the trip with them, and each one came to a different conclusion, a conclusion that was firmer than just a personal opinion. Uniform and total agreement is not always going to be the outcome, even when the Spirit of God is present and even when what is at stake is a timeless truth.

Another example can be found in 1 Corinthians 10. In this epistle the apostle Paul gets into a rhetorical discussion with the people of Corinth concerning the practice of eating meat that had been offered to idols. In the conversation various viewpoints are offered on both sides of the issue. The question up for discussion is this: Can we eat meat offered to idols? "Everything is permissible" (1 Cor. 10:23) is Paul's first response. After all, the redeemed of Corinth know idols were really just pieces of stone. Undoubtedly there were people in the Corinthian Christian community who delighted in eating the fresh meat. They didn't care that it had been blessed at the temple of a pagan god. The Spirit had led them to have clear consciences about it. In fact, Paul tends to agree. "Eat anything sold in the meat market without raising questions of conscience, for 'the earth is the Lord's, and everything in it'" (1 Cor. 10:25–26). Paul quotes a mealtime prayer that Jews used (Ps. 24:1). If the Spirit leads a person to perceive these verses as timeless truths then there is no reason to worry about what to eat. The Spirit has led them to their clear consciences.

There are others who, upon reading this same text, might be led by the Spirit to put the emphasis on a different part of it. "'Everything is permissible' but not everything is constructive. Nobody should seek his own good, but the good of others" (1 Cor. 10:23–24). For these folks, the Spirit leads them to see the text as indicating that they should be aware of who they are with before indulging in their freedom. Here's a modern application of this interpretation. Imagine a pastor who enjoys bringing beer on church council retreats. It is a totally permissible practice in his denomination and, in fact, is a tradition of that particular congregation. In the past, the group has gathered at a lake-side cabin, completed their church business, and then relaxed with a few beers and conversation before calling it a night. That was the standard until one year, when a fellow who was a recovering alcoholic joined the church council. When the new council member finished sharing his testimony, one of the veteran members of the council asked him how he felt about the group drinking beers after the meeting. The recovering alcoholic graciously said that it didn't bother him. The wise veteran council member then suggested that he, too, could finish the retreat without a beer, and he asked if anybody else cared to join him in abstaining. One by one the other members of the council adopted a no-drinking policy for the rest of their retreats.

Yes, they as a council were free to drink beer. After all, not everyone in the group had an alcohol problem. However, the Spirit led this particular council to come to the conclusion they'd use their freedom to support their new member's recovery. In an act of solidarity with him they chose as a group to abstain from using alcohol on the retreat. As individuals, most council members felt free to drink. As a council, the Spirit led them to a sensitivity that they had not displayed before. This is an example of the same freedom used in two different ways. When the Spirit leads, people can choose to follow.

In 1 Corinthians the apostle Paul is forced to deal with the human inclination to divide rather than live together agreeing to disagree. He says, "I appeal to you, brothers, in the name of our Lord Jesus Christ, that all of you agree with one another so that there may be no divisions among you and that you may be perfectly united in mind and thought." Obviously the members of the church in Corinth were not of one mind. In fact, later in the chapter Paul notes that the congregation in Corinth was breaking into groups, one that followed Apollos, one that followed Cephas, another that followed Paul, and one that just looked to Christ. Yes, the human temptation to build differentiating walls and to stay behind those walls is as old as humanity itself. Paul goes on to ask an important question: "Is Christ divided?" The rhetorical question begs for the answer no, Christ is not divided. Yet, Christ's body on earth (the church) was fragmenting then and it has been prone to dividing ever since. Why does the body of Christ on earth continually divide? I think it is because followers of Jesus have a difficult time accepting that one Spirit can lead different people to different conclusions on any given text or topic. As I have attempted to show throughout this book, the library we call the Bible is filled with verses that are in tension with one another. They do not agree. Conflicting texts that are made into timeless truths by opposing individuals or groups often give rise to hard choices, choices that have had to be justified and enforced.

An example might be a woman who has grown up in the Roman Catholic tradition and who feels a calling from the Spirit of God to go into full-time ministry: she discerns the call to be a priest. Having experienced the grace of God, she feels empowered by the Spirit, called and gifted to be a priest. She applies to the nearest Catholic seminary. In essence, the Spirit leads her and she presents her building plans to the zoning commission of the theological neighborhood in which she lives. But the zoning committee of that theological neighborhood does not approve her plan. She is the wrong gender. The timeless truth texts held by the Catholic Church only allow men to become priests. Although she feels led by the Spirit to be a priest, the diocese feels led by the Spirit and tradition that she cannot serve God in that way. The two sides are in tension with one another. She is now faced with several options. One: she can curse the Church for such an inflexible stance, reject taking up the kind of spiritual life the Spirit of God has suggested altogether, and live in an attitude of frustration. This is certainly a common human response to disappointment and feelings of rejection. However, is that where the Spirit of God would take her? A second option would be this: she could accept the decision of her neighborhood zoning commission and look into building a house whose plans they would approve. That is, she could pursue the spiritual vocations that are available to her as a woman within that particular tradition. Or if she feels led by the Spirit to consider a third option, she might do this: she could seek a different theological neighborhood, a faith community that has a building code permitting women to pursue ordination. If she feels compelled by the Spirit she could seek to build her theological house in that new location thus fulfilling the call she has felt on her life.

These options for following the Spirit's lead may arise in another circumstance as well. Let's consider a young man who feels called into ministry but has to struggle with what to do about his same-gender orientation. Should he follow the U.S. military approach of just not saying anything or not telling anyone until after he is ordained? Should he contain his sexual urges and follow any of the three traditional grace approaches, options that would allow him to serve as a pastor as long as he does not act on his sexuality? Should he claim realist radical grace and hold himself accountable to the same standards of moral conduct of his heterosexual seminary classmates? Eventually he will have to present his life building plans to the theological neighborhood in which he hopes to live and serve. Those assessing the neighborhood plans in turn will either approve his plan or reject it based on whichever Bible verses they have put in place as internal walls of timeless truth. If the neighborhood he pursues is predominantly inhabited by traditional grace thinkers, the young man will need to face conforming to their expectations of celibacy or face having his call rejected. If the community he wants to serve is of the Radical Grace persuasion, then he may be permitted to be in a committed relationship and use his gifts to serve the body of Christ. Either neighborhood will issue building permits based on their particular combination of timeless truth texts. It will be up to the young man to follow the Spirit's lead and to conform to the zoning ordinances of the neighborhood he chooses to pursue. As you can see, both of these situations will be influenced by the verses the zoning commissions place as timeless truths.

Are there situations in which congregations of the same denomination can coexist with different timeless truth texts? I believe it is possible. For example, one church might hold to the traditional grace timeless truth texts and the other church the realist radical grace timeless truth texts. Both congregations have firm foundations and frameworks of unshakable grace. Each believes that the same sacraments dispense God's grace in tangible form. The members of each congregation share a common concern for reaching the whole world with the good news of God's love, Jesus' forgiveness, and the Holy Spirit's power. Each congregation is committed to enacting the tangible marks of discipleship to Jesus through worship, study, prayer, fellowship, and service to the world. With so many important things in common, why would the body of Christ feel the need to divide over one particular issue? There is no need for such a split if both congregations accept that their zoning ordinances are only slightly different, if both congregations can accept that the same Holy Spirit has led each of them to a different conclusion on a given subject. If the Spirit of God is allowed to lead, then each congregation can celebrate their shared foundation of grace, they can appreciate their similar goal of building God's kingdom on earth and they can agree to disagree on the zoning ordinances that mark their differences.

In such mutual respect, Christ's body on earth is honored. The Spirit alone can create what Peter describes when he says, "Above all, love each other deeply, because love covers over a multitude of sins. Offer hospitality to one another without grumbling. Each one should use whatever gift he has received to serve others, faithfully administering God's grace in its various forms. If anyone speaks, he should do it as one speaking the very words of God. If anyone serves, he should do it with the strength God provides, so that in all things God may be praised through Jesus Christ. To him be the glory and the power for ever and ever. Amen" (1 Pet. 4:8–11). This is a timeless truth worth pursuing.

© Yanik Chauvin | Dreamstime.com

Grace *in Action*

I believe the gospel of grace is the weight-bearing frame of every house of biblical interpretation. Therefore, the gospel of grace is the most important concept to be communicated. As a pastor I am always looking for helpful sermon illustrations with the aim of recasting Bible stories in such a way as to make them more understandable and real. I would like to share a couple of my favorite stories that help make the gospel of grace more obvious.

Grace and a canoe. As a youngster, I lived in a faith community that sponsored a summer youth camp. I loved going every year. We had a couple traditions at camp that were as predictable as the sun rising every day. The first tradition was spending some time canoeing on a creek that was not far from the camp in eastern Pennsylvania. The best part of that activity was the water wars we would have at the end of the day. We splashed water on each other and ultimately tried to tip the other canoes over. Victory went to the last canoe team floating.

The second tradition was a closing campfire held on the last night of the week. These yearly campfire nights tended to end up being pretty emotional. The speaker would summarize the week by asking all of us campers assembled around the tower of burning wood if we wanted to commit our lives to Jesus. The first year, I was excited to give my life to Jesus. We were encouraged to go home and live for Jesus. I sure wanted to do that, at least to the best of my ability.

The next summer I returned to camp and sure enough, on campfire night we were given the same opportunity to give our lives to Jesus. I was thinking I had already done that, but the speaker asked us if we had sinned in the last year. Of course, we all had. In that case, he said, we needed to give our lives to Jesus again. At the time I felt a little confused; I thought I was already saved. But here was the speaker asking me to recommit my life to Jesus, and if I didn't commit to Jesus and if I died on the way home, I might not spend eternity in heaven. Wow, I thought. I better give my life to Jesus again. I didn't want to risk spending eternity in hellish flames like the huge yellow and orange ones crackling in front of us on the campgrounds. So once again I gave my life to Jesus.

By year three, campfire night evoked feelings of frustration. Yes, I had sinned over the course of the year. But when the speaker asked us to give our lives to Jesus again I wanted to know why Jesus' grace from last year wasn't enough to cover this year's sin. Where had Jesus' grace gone? Did he forget my sincere commitment last year and the year before? Out of fear and some guilt, I yet again committed my life to Jesus. But I had more questions. God's grace seemed to be an illusive thing. It would only be years later that I put my camp experience into perspective. And surprisingly enough, it was the canoe trek every week at camp that gave me the insight I had been seeking for so many years.

As a pastor on one of these camping summer weeks, I was asked by a parishioner if we could ever lose God's grace. I smiled and thought about my own youthful wonderment at the same question. I believe that it was then that the Holy Spirit brought my canoe and campfire experiences together and gave me an answer I have used ever since. I start by suggesting we are born floating in the lake of life. We do not want to drown so we try and try on our own to stay afloat. God in his mercy builds a canoe called grace. The canoe is a gift that floats out to us. We cannot buy the canoe, and we cannot build it for ourselves. Only God can build it. Furthermore, we can choose to get into the canoe of grace or we can ignore it. We enter the canoe of grace through our baptism into Jesus Christ. Now, as a Lutheran, I believe that parents can put their child in the canoe of grace through the baptism of their children at any age. Obviously, adults who were not baptized as infants can also choose to get into the canoe of grace whenever they choose to be baptized into Christ. But we still might ask, once in the canoe of grace, can a person fall out?

I realized that as a kid at camp, every summer I was getting into the canoe of God's grace. And then every year, I perceived that my sinful actions would force the canoe to capsize and I was in the water again. Every summer I would have to choose to climb back into the canoe and worry that sometime during the upcoming year I would overturn the canoe and be back in the water, fighting for my life again. This outlook made God's grace seem very tenuous. I never felt secure, as I thought that the canoe of grace was not stable. I wasn't sure at what point the sin in my life would throw me back into the water and I would need to seek God's grace again. Obviously, camp was one place where I realized the need for God's grace year after year.

In contrast to my youthful understanding, today I believe God's canoe of grace is very stable. In fact, nothing on the lake of life can force us out of the canoe. When we climb into the canoe of God's grace, we are secure for eternity. Once we are in the canoe, we will not drown. I wish I had felt that security when I was a kid. But I feel it now, thanks be to God.

Once we are in the canoe of grace we have some additional choices. We can choose to learn the J-stroke or build a sail with a paddle and tarp. In other words, we can learn to be intentional about how we live and use the canoe of grace. This is what I would call sanctification. Having received God's grace in the form of the canoe, we can work out how to best use the canoe as an expression of thanks to God for putting us in this special, secure place. On the other hand, we can choose to do nothing special. Some folks just float in their canoe and make no effort to understand or appreciate all they could do with it. As they choose to ignore the grace, some may even choose to continually sin. This does not cause the canoe to overturn. They are still in God's canoe of grace, something that has been a source of comfort for some and encouragement for others. God's grace does not disappear just because we are imperfect.

My parishioner, upon hearing my explanation, then asked if there is any circumstance whereby a person can fall out of the canoe of God's grace. I have made Matthew 12:32 a timeless truth in my house of biblical interpretation. It reads "Anyone who speaks a word against the Son of Man will be forgiven, but anyone who speaks against the Holy Spirit will not be forgiven, either in this age or in the age to come." Can a person choose to jump out of the canoe? Matthew seems to suggest that blaspheming the Holy Spirit may be the one thing a person can do to jump out of the canoe of grace. Please note: the person has to jump out of the canoe on purpose. God does not overturn the canoe. Ever. No sin seems to cause the canoe to overturn. What an incredible act of love God's canoe of grace is for all who climb into it through their baptism into Christ.

Jonah and the Packers. Jonah lived in south Minneapolis. Jonah was a prophet of God. He was also a diehard Minnesota Viking football fan. He loved the purple-and-gold warriors who did battle every fall weekend on the turf of the Hubert H. Humphrey Metrodome. As a died-in-the wool Viking fan, Jonah grew up hating the Green Bay Packers. Those hideous green-and-yellow uniforms were the bane of his existence. The weekends that the Packers and Vikings did battle were the most emotional of the entire season. In fact, for Jonah, any season was a success if the Vikings beat the Packers.

One weekend Jonah received a message from God. Jonah was told to go to Green Bay's Lambeau Field and announce to the crowd that God wanted to include them in his kingdom. Jonah was appalled. How can this be? Because Jonah hated the Packer-backers he had assumed God hated them, too. But God was insistent that Jonah go to Green Bay and announce that the gospel of grace was available to all the cheese heads in Wisconsin.

Jonah had an internal struggle with the assignment. And after thinking about it for a day, he defiantly chose to head west, away from Minneapolis and in the opposite direction of Green Bay. About the time Jonah got to Sioux Falls, South Dakota, God created a huge ice storm that forced all the traffic to come to a slip-sliding stop. As Jonah sat in the storm, he realized that the storm was his fault. God had created an obstacle that stopped him from getting farther away from his assignment. It was then that Jonah owned his disobedience to God's command. As an act of repentance he was put on an eastbound Greyhound bus and for three days they slowly made their way across the southern part of Minnesota and then across western and central Wisconsin.

It was a fateful Sunday afternoon when the reluctant prophet walked on to Lambeau Field. As he looked around at the thousands of green and yellow clad fans he whispered in a small voice, "God loves you and wants to include you in his kingdom." Jonah hoped that no one would hear him. Jonah really hoped none of them would accept the grace that God was offering. Much to his amazement and disappointment, the Packer throng heard the good news of the gospel and accepted it. They were redeemed that day and all who accepted the message were included in the kingdom of God.

Jonah was so depressed that he went out into the parking lot and wanted to die.

If you read the Hebrew Testament story of Jonah, you see God wanted to include in his kingdom a city, Nineveh, that Jonah did not want to see saved. How often God seeks to be more inclusive than the messengers he sends!

Grace on a Lake. Moving to Minnesota as an adult meant that I never learned a number of Upper Midwest skills that most people learn as kids. One was water skiing on one ski, an activity known as slaloming. As an adult, I learned how to water ski on two skis just fine, but mastering the balance needed to have both feet on one ski was a real challenge. One Saturday we were at our family lake cabin and the weather was perfect for water skiing. I decided to give up my usual duty as boat driver and give skiing another chance. My wife took over as the boat's driver and one of our kids served as spotter. Upon my giving the proper gesture, the boat raced forward and I was up and out of the water, skiing comfortably on two skis. As we made our way around the perimeter of the lake I was feeling really good. As we approached the spot where we usually dropped off I got the idea of trying to drop the right ski and give slaloming another shot. I had no way of mentioning my intention to anyone; it was a spur-of-the-moment decision that only I knew about. As my wife zoomed toward our dock and made the sharp turn, a move that would normally send me to a safe stop by the beach, I chose to drop the right ski. Much to everyone's surprise, and especially mine, I did not fall over. In fact, I successfully positioned my right foot behind my left foot on the one ski: I was slaloming! What a thrill. I was weaving my way over the wake of the boat having a grand time when I tried to cut a turn too sharply and went down. But I didn't care. I had successfully slalomed for the first time in my life.

As my wife made the turn to come back and pick me up she was stopped by a water patrol boat. I was bobbing in the water watching a conversation I could not hear. After several minutes I saw the water patrol officer write up a ticket and hand it to my wife. When the boat finally came to get me, I asked what was going on. I was then informed that I had just received a seventy-five-dollar fine. "For what?" I shouted. It seems that we had broken a state law. When the boat went through the dock area at full throttle it is required that the skier drop off. My choosing to stay on meant the boat had gone too fast within one hundred feet of shore. So we got a misdemeanor speeding fine of seventy-five dollars. At first I was mad at the water patrol person for wrecking my euphoric experience. Then I was mad at the dumb rule. Finally I realized I should be angry with myself.

When we got back to shore we explained to my inquisitive mother-in-law the reason we had been floating in the middle of the lake for fifteen minutes. I was appropriately remorseful knowing that I was going to be seventy-five dollars poorer when we mailed in the check. Then unexpectedly, grace hit.

Out of the blue my mother-in-law said, "I'll pay the fine." "What?" I responded. "That's not necessary; my mistake, my consequence." I had preached that idea to our four kids for years. She, however, had made up her mind. "I'll pay it. Period." I have learned over the years that my mother-in-law is a woman of resolve. What she says she is going to do she does. There it was: grace in action. My mistake, her willingness to pay it on my behalf. Did I deserve such a reprieve? No. Did I expect it? No; it was just given.

So, too, with God's grace. Deserved? No. Freely given? You bet. It comes to us. We have all sinned and fallen short of God's instructions for living a good life. We have all received misdemeanor tickets. However, God steps in and pays the fine, giving us undeserved, unexpected grace that covers our personal ticket.

I encourage you to think about experiences in your life when you have known the unmerited favor of others or of God. I invite you to make a list of times, people, and places when grace was shown to you or you gave grace to someone else. These are important memories to preserve. To communicate God's incredible grace is the reason the library we call the Bible was assembled.

Here are fifteen key terms used in this book:

literalist: An individual who believes the Bible is without mistakes (i.e., is inerrant), is inspired by God, and must be interpreted at face value. The words mean what they say and most texts are to be understood literally

selectivist: An individual who believes the Bible is the inspired Word of God, but who accepts that some verses are to be taken literally while other verses are not to be taken at face value. These folks often perceive some texts to be more important than others.

domino theory: This hermeneutical approach suggests that if one verse of the Bible is proven to be wrong then a domino effect could take place , which undermines the authority of the entire Bible.

house theory: This hermeneutical approach is based on the belief that changes in biblical interpretation can be done without undermining the credibility of the entire Bible. The frame of the house is the gospel of grace; the distinct internal walls are made of timeless truths; the decorating and color schemes are the cultural norms and personal opinions of the Bible reader; and the unusual decorations we do not know what to do with are the random texts of the Bible. The house theory suggests that rooms in a house of biblical interpretation can be redecorated or remodeled without the house falling down.

gospel of grace: Grace is the goodwill and favor shown to one who can plead no merit to receiving it from God. The gospel of grace is found equally in the Hebrew and Greek Testaments. God's grace takes multiple forms and is offered to people regardless of their gender, nationality, language group, education, or economic status.

timeless truths: These are the verses in the Bible chosen to be important. They help define what a person, church, or denomination believes is necessary in order to be in right relationship with God. The verses put in this category carry with them the expectation that the person holding them would also choose to live by them.

cultural norms: These are the verses that individuals, churches, and denominations use to determine the practices that define them as a cultural group. Cultural norms are unique to each group and often subject to conversation and debate among members of groups.

personal opinions: These are the verses that the author of any given text in the Bible attributes to his own thoughts, experiences, biases, or perspectives. Personal opinions are subject to change when new insights, information, or situations present themselves.

random texts: These are Bible verses that just do not seem to fit easily into any message the Bible seems to send. They are found in both the Hebrew and Greek Testaments. These verses raise more questions than answers.

old school logic: This approach was originally called deuteronomist thinking. The main precepts are that if you obey God, then you will be blessed; if you disobey God, then you will be punished. Examples are found in both the Hebrew and Greek Testaments.

realist logic: This approach was originally called non-deuteronomist thinking. The main precept is that life is lived, and that good and bad events happen randomly to both good and bad people. A person does not have to look for meaning behind every random occurrence

inclusivist: This thinking suggests that God seeks to include everyone in his kingdom.

exclusivist: This thinking holds that not everyone will be included in the kingdom of God. Only those who conform to the prescribed verses, beliefs, and lifestyle expectations will be saved.

traditional grace: This is the belief that God's redeeming grace is dependent on individuals conforming to the correct beliefs, attitudes, and lifestyle actions that are prescribed in selected texts of the Bible.

realist radical grace: This is the belief that God's grace is given to whomever God chooses. It is not necessarily predictable and is extended to any individual God has made clean

Acknowledgements

I am grateful for a number of professors from my first seminary experience who began opening the Bible to me in ways that I had not previously experienced. Dr. Bob Guelich and Dr. Berkeley Mickelsen each made the Greek Testament come to life in ways that stretched my imagination. I am also grateful that members of the Colonial Church of Edina, Minnesota, entrusted their teenagers to the long-haired, motorcycle-riding youth director from the East. I am especially thankful for the teenagers of Pilgrim Fellowship (PF) who gathered in incredible numbers to influence their peers about faith. We always said that the number of people who show up indicates a group's popularity at the moment; where people are in their faith five and ten years later determines a group's effectiveness. (I think this is still true for churches as well.) I have been inspired by the many young people from PF who have matured into men and women and who have established families of faith.

I am grateful for the wonderful people of St. Andrew's Lutheran Church in Mahtomedi, Minnesota, who gathered to study God's word in deep ways. They asked great questions and they endured borderline heretical conversations, but in the end, the Spirit of God led us to an understanding of how people might gather around the scriptures. Together we learned that God's word is a living document, that we do not have to agree about every interpretation, that the Spirit can lead each of us to a different conclusion, and that we can nevertheless have loving and encouraging conversations. We often commented that "in unison" was not the only way a song could be sung. In fact, most of us preferred singing and listening to voices in harmony, with sopranos, altos, tenors, and basses each singing different notes (hopefully, on the same page of the same song!) but blending together to make the music interesting. So, too, with biblical interpretation. We do not all have to have one voice (and so be in unison) about every text. There may be passages of the Bible to which we assign different notes, yet it is in the harmonizing of the different interpretations that the sweet melody of salvation is heard. Regardless of how we may interpret a given text, the same God loves us, the same Jesus forgives us, and the same Spirit guides and empowers us.

I am grateful for the incredible members and friends of Community Lutheran Church in Las Vegas, Nevada. Not only were they bold enough to call me as their pastor, but they also enabled me to take the time to write this book. I have appreciated the staff allowing me my Wednesday afternoons of uninterrupted study and writing. I also have been encouraged by the interest of church members and the questions they have asked as we have used the tools of this book in both the teaching and preaching in our church. Some folks have wondered, can anything spiritual come out of "Sin City"? You bet! (Pun intended.) God has frequently used unexpected times and places to communicate important timeless truths. Who would have guessed two thousand years ago that the first-century version of "Sin City," Corinth, would be the place where arguably the most quoted text of the Bible would first be directed. Yet, for over two millennia 1 Corinthians 13 has told us what love is and what it is not. So our modern version of "Sin City" may one day have a similar distinction. It remains to be seen whether this book will play any part in that, but one of my hopes is that it will.

I am especially grateful for the expert assistance of the folks at Beaver's Pond Press. They helped to make this project a reality. Thanks go to Joe Moses who served as my executive editor and to Jennifer Manion who served as my copyeditor. Thanks to Rick Korab of Punch Design for the cover design and layout of the book, and my appreciation to Jen Allen for ideas about the format. Thanks to Robin Martelli who transcribed lectures onto written pages. Thanks too to Fred Harmon, Greg Davis, Diane Nelson, Arsenia Walker, Jim Anderson, Ryan Alexander, Bonnie Montesano, and Squire Rushnell…who read portions or all of the manuscript and offered me feedback.

And finally, thanks to all of you who have chosen to read this book. I hope and pray that the tools offered will assist you in gaining a more positive understanding of the library we call the Bible. God's blessings to you all.

— *Mark Wickstrom*

NOTES